UNDERSTANDING RELIGION

UNDERSTANDING RELIGION

Eric J. Sharpe
Professor of Religious Studies in the University of Sydney

Duckworth

Second impression 1988
First published in 1983 by
Gerald Duckworth and Company Ltd.,
The Old Piano Factory,
43 Gloucester Crescent, London NW1

ISBN 0 7156 1657 9 (cased)
ISBN 0 7156 1735 4 (paper)

British Library Cataloguing in Publication Data

Sharpe, Eric
Understanding religion.
1. Religion
I. Title
200 BL48

ISBN 0 7156 1657 9

Photoset in North Wales by
Derek Doyle & Associates, Mold, Clwyd
Printed in Great Britain by
Redwood Burn Limited, Trowbridge

Contents

To adore, or scorne an image, or protest
May all be bad; doubt wisely; in strange way
To stand inquiring right, is not to stray;
To sleepe, or runne wrong, is.

John Donne

Ce n'est pas dans les possibilités, c'est dans
l'homme même qu'il faut étudier l'homme: il ne s'agit
pas d'imaginer ce qu'il auroit pû ou dû faire, mais
de regarder ce qu'il fait.

Charles De Brosses

Preface

This book sets out to explore some of the implications of the study of religion. It is not however a catalogue of 'religions', that is, of the various more or less organised ways in which human beings have reacted to the supra-sensory aspect of the universe. It is rather an inquiry into the presuppositions of the study itself. Nor does it offer any systematic account of the commonly accepted 'methods' used by scholars working in this field. Although I hope eventually to write such a book – not least because I believe it to be both instructive and important to know how theologians, historians, philosophers, psychologists, phenomenologists and others try to organize and deal with the material under their hand, this is not my present intention. Here I am concerned with the initial approach to religion as a field of study, with the ground that needs to be cleared, the difficulties that need to be faced and at least some of the personal, as well as the technical, questions that may arise as the study proceeds.

In what follows I shall use the term 'religious studies' fairly frequently, but it may be as well to admit at the outset that, in doing so, I am in a sense flying a flag of convenience. No one has yet come up with an entirely satisfactory short form of words to describe the type of study discussed in these pages. In trying to describe it one generally has to resort to a collection of ponderous compound words – multi-cultural, non-confessional and inter-disciplinary, among others – and this may perhaps be taken as a sign of the difficulties which are involved. 'Religious studies' is admittedly not ideal, but it is by now fairly common. Although I was brought up on the older term 'comparative religion', and a few years ago argued for its retention (Sharpe, 1975: xiii f.), I make little use of it in this book, mainly because most people still suppose that it means the study of every religion *except* Christianity (in the same way that they generally assume that the interchangeable terms 'divinity' and 'theology' refer *only* to the study of Christianity). Words may of course be redefined, but there seems little point in fighting against these compact linguistic conventions.

The trouble with 'religious studies' is the adjectival use of the word 'religious'. We speak of 'religious drama' and 'religious music', 'religious behaviour' and 'religious ritual', and mean that each is shaped by a quality of devotion or by 'religious experience'. To call someone 'a religious' means that he lives his life under sacred vows. 'Religious' in these cases therefore means the taking on of a certain character and the acceptance of certain functions which religion itself determines in advance. This is not however the sense in which today's educationalists use the expression 'religious studies' (though there have been those who have objected to its educational use for precisely these reasons, and have suggested alternatives, such as 'studies in religion'). In present-day parlance, the term may be taken to mean 'studies in and around the phenomena associated with religion'. Admittedly, it is not ideal; but it is generally understood, and that may perhaps suffice. But let us be quite clear on one point: that in principle, 'religious studies' excludes nothing identifiable as belonging within the category of 'religion'. How the identification is to be carried out we shall consider in due course.

Normally when the student, either privately or in school, college or university, embarks on a course of religious studies (or whatever else it may be called), he or she will begin with collections of 'facts about the world's religions', read and digested in a certain conventional order. Of the making of books containing such facts there appears to be no end. Some are better than others, but most are within their given limits reasonably informative. A further stage may be the reading of a book on the *history* of the study of religions: having written such a book myself (*Comparative Religion: A History*, 1975), it would be foolish of me to deny the practical usefulness of the 'history of ideas' approach which it represents. But where the student may often be left to flounder is in the matter of how to approach and digest the material. Is it possible to set bounds to what is religion, and what is not? Have the geographically and historically oriented textbooks said all that need be said about the nature of the material, and the sources from which it comes? How might that material be grouped and classified? And what of the student's own personal and private religious concerns – all those beliefs, assumptions, preferences and antipathies which are sometimes expressed publicly, sometimes nursed in private, but which the study of religion cannot but touch? Are these to play a part in the process of study or are they not? Every teacher of religion, whether in school, college, seminary or university, knows that the learning process may be a traumatic one, and remembers students who broke under the strain. Can anything be done, if not to eliminate, at least to anticipate the shock?

As a rule the textbooks of religious studies remain stubbornly silent on questions like these, and even those which claim to tackle the study of religion as a whole usually do little more than provide new permutations and combinations of already well-known material. In what follows, I have attempted to formulate and carry through a different approach, one in which the student's motivation and possible questions and difficulties have been temporarily elevated above the cataloguing of the actual material studied, and above an account of the various methods which might be applied in the course of study.

I am making three assumptions, which I shall attempt to state clearly at the very outset. The first is that the area of 'religion' is capable of being, if not strictly defined, at least outlined as a field of study. The second is that the study has an intrinsic value of its own, which is not necessarily bound up with the stated or assumed goals of religious commitment as such. The third is an extension of the second, and is an assumption that this study can be undertaken without applying the criteria of 'truth' and/or 'falsehood' to any of the material under consideration.

That religion is capable of being studied because, like iron ore or Mount Everest, it is simply *there* as a part of human experience, is an intellectual position which many find surprisingly difficult to grasp. Because religion is admittedly bound up with such matters as 'faith', 'belief' and 'commitment', what (it is asked) can be the purpose of study if not to deepen the faith, belief and commitment one already possesses? Will not the study of religion 'in the round' inevitably lead to the rejection of all that does not square with one's preconceived notions on the subject? Are not all religious assumptions, statements, doctrines and dogmas necessarily either 'true' or 'false'? How then can the student avoid constantly having to make up his mind and take up a personal stance on every individual issue as it arises?

Wilfred Cantwell Smith once wrote that '[r]eligious truth is utterly crucial; is the paramount and inescapable issue, before which all other religious matters, however mighty, must bow. It is final.' (Smith, 1967: 67). This sounds – indeed is – utterly uncompromising. But at the same time Smith was not saying that 'religions' contain collections of 'truths' (or what are claimed to be so): rather he was stressing that truth *becomes* true only as it is appropriated by the individual and bears its fruits. This is not a matter of accepting some religious statements as true and rejecting others as false, but of apprehending what the different religious traditions have to teach, and of allowing those apprehensions to shape one's life.

This view does not solve all the difficulties which the student of religion faces, but it does suggest that the range of possibilities is greater than many of the separate traditions allow. If the student remains within the light-and-darkness, life-and-death, truth-and-falsehood pattern of *one* religious tradition, then the alternatives must be those stated in the Book of Deuteronomy (30: 15, 19): 'See, I have set before you this day life and good, death and evil ... I have set before you life and death, blessing and curse; therefore choose life ...'

But the student of religion (as opposed, perhaps, to the adept or to the student of theology) does not necessarily fit into this uncompromising pattern. As a rule he will be different in two respects. First, he is working not within one religious tradition, but many, perhaps ranging all the way from the shamanism of the Eskimo to the esotericism of the Zen Buddhist, from the pomp of the mediaeval Catholic cathedral to the simplicity of the Quaker meeting-house. Secondly, he is painting on a canvas which is as vast as human history, in length as well as breadth. On it Thor and Odin, Osiris and Horus, Varuna and Mitra share the scene with Yahweh, Allah and the ineffable Brahman. To speak of making a simple existential choice between what is 'true' and what is 'false' in this immense panorama may be possible, given certain presuppositions; for a certain type of mind it may be fascinating. But it is not inevitable.

An analogy – though doubtless inadequate – may serve to illustrate the point. In the world there are many languages, and most human beings are born into an area in which only one of them is spoken: to the average person, that language will be his 'mother tongue', in which he moves freely, and expressed himself with ease and confidence. In time, he may learn other languages, and may attain a considerable degree of fluency in one or more of them. He may subsequently enter into the academic discipline of linguistics, and form theories concerning the structure and function of 'language-as-such' on a basis of what he already knows of specific languages. But although his mother-tongue will still be English, Swedish, Tamil or Swahili, there is no reason why he should be tempted to range languages on an ascending scale of value, or to classify languages into categories of 'true' and 'false'. His criteria will be functional rather than normative, and however different languages may be, there remains for the student the overriding concern of the way in which each functions as a medium of human communication. Just as linguistics serves to deal with these questions on a wide front, so 'religious studies' is able to deal with structure and function in the area of religion, leaving more controversial matters aside.

It follows (and this may be harder to grasp) that the student of religion is in most cases engaged on a different quest from that which motivates the spiritual pilgrim. His quest is an intellectual quest for explanations which do not do violence to profound convictions, and not a spiritual quest for deepened commitment (though this is not to say that the two may not overlap). He is seeking to grasp human motivation, reactions to the ultimate mysteries of human existence, human hopes, joys, fears and failures, beginnings and ends. He is not in the first instance trying to make himself more or less 'religious', though he may have reason to believe that there exist in himself the 'religious' qualities he observes in others. He may reflect on others' 'truth-claims' (as they have come to be called), but if in the last analysis he believes any particular religious statement to be true, he will hold this belief in abeyance. Whether or not a statement is true is to the working student less important than that there is a phenomenon of belief and action to be observed, understood and explained. This particular quest some may consider a deliberate (and perhaps even a shameful) avoidance of the divine imperative. For the scholar, though, the attempt to explain is a quest having its own integrity, perhaps not too far removed from the desire to reach the regions of ultimate truth.

The study of religion in the sense in which it is discussed in these pages is, therefore, a behavioural science (or art, or craft). It is first of all the study of human beings feeling, thinking and behaving in a certain way or ways, both as individuals and as groups. These feelings, thoughts and habits can, of course, be studied with a view to their acceptability, to their reasonableness or unreasonableness, and to their conformity to other habits of human thought and behaviour. They may be – though they need not necessarily be – compared with one another in such a way as to show up similarities, differences and distinctive features generally. In every case, though, the student has to remember that every belief, every doctrine, every ritual, every myth is or has been part of the mental equipment of living and breathing human beings. In a word, the student is studying *people*, and not quaint abstractions. Because the study of religion is the study of people (not all of whom are dead), and because the student is part of that which he is studying, the subject at the very least possesses human interest, and if pursued with a measure of dedication, is capable of providing valuable (even though often ignored) insights into human motivation and human conduct in its totality. Speaking of the dialogue which emerges in the study of religion between western and other religions and cultures, Mircea Eliade writes that '[t]he history of religions and religious ethnology are of a much more urgent usefulness in the politics of today than are economics or sociology' (Eliade, 1978: 117). This is so precisely because the study leads beyond the superficialities of social machinery into the vast and complex hinterland of human motivation. It may do even more than this, and many of those who study or have studied religion would maintain that it *does* do more, by giving the student an insight into the deepest secrets of the universe, and into the ways in which Omnipotence (or Ultimate Reality) has been apprehended by the world. But this is by no means inevitable, and there have been many students who have preferred to limit their studies to the human face of religion, shying away from the deepest and most difficult questions.

By the very nature of things, of course, the existence or otherwise of any supernatural being cannot be finally and conclusively demonstrated by any kind of rational proof. Our human reason operates only on the evidence fed to it from the senses; and, by definition, the supernatural does not and cannot fully conform to sensory criteria. Even if it were to express itself through means belonging to the sensory world (by talking, becoming visible, or throwing teacups) still there would be no conclusive reasons why such manifestations had come from *outside* the world of the senses –

precisely the reason why spiritualists have always found the workaday world so lamentably hard to convince of the reality of psychic phenomena. Even the evidence of 'altered states of consciousness' brought about in dreams, periods of sickness, in trances and by the influence of hallucinogenic drugs, though they may be *interpreted* as pointing to an alternative state of Being (or at least as setting bounds on normality), do not conclusively *prove* the existence of that state of Being. Those who believe that the evidence adds up to conclusive proof do so as a rule on other grounds entirely, and are using the evidence to confirm a view they already hold. In most cases, therefore, absolute rational conviction is not something that can be attained apart from the prior exercise of some form of faith. It involves, in William James' term, 'the will to believe'; and unless that will can be brought into play, purely rational argument is as ineffective as torture as a means of persuasion.

In most cases, therefore, the study of religion will almost inevitably confirm or support whatever attitude the student already holds concerning the ultimate object of study. Equally, in most cases our subject is less the study of God (theology) than a specialised aspect of anthropology, concerned specifically with the ways in which human beings have reacted to, and drawn theoretical and practical conclusions from, the idea of God, the gods, or Ultimate Reality.

Whichever course the student may take – irrespective of whether he or she regards religion as a response to divine revelation or merely as an expression of the workings of the human heart and mind and imagination – it remains entirely feasible to study the ideas and the patterns of behaviour to which it gives rise. Whether or not all human beings think and believe, it is an elementary observation that all human beings behave, and one cannot proceed very far in the study of human behaviour without noticing that in most parts of the world, and in most periods of human history, people have behaved as though their lives had some final point of reference and responsibility outside themselves. Often the deepest springs of human action have been found in precisely this area – the strongest convictions, the most profound commitments, the heights and the depths of human experience.

This being so – and even the one who does not actually approve of religion would find this general conclusion hard to avoid – then the study of religion becomes not only a diversion, but a necessity for anyone who claims an interest in human behaviour. For the one under the pressure of the divine imperative, for the committed believer of whatever creed or community, the need is still more pressing, even though there are reasons (which we shall examine in due course) why the subject matter may be more circumscribed, and the student's attitude of mind different. Perhaps the conditions governing the latter's work may have unduly influenced the former. That again is a matter to which we shall return. Let us say at this stage only that the study of religion can be, and ought to be, both fruitful and exciting, without necessarily being easy. If the pages which follow suceed at least in communicating some of the fascination which I myself have found in a quarter of a century of study in this area, I will feel amply rewarded.

*

Some of the material on which this book is based has from time to time been presented to students in the Universities of Lancaster and Sydney in lectures and seminars. On this occasion, however, it has been shorn of most of its illustrations. To have illustrated every point would have caused it to expand beyond the range suited to the students for whom it is chiefly intended. For the same reason I have excluded all but the most unavoidable references.

My friends and colleagues John R. Hinnells and Lennart Ståhle have read various parts of the initial draft, and I thank them for their comments and criticisms.

I dedicate the book as a whole to my colleagues and students in the Department of Religious Studies of the University of Sydney.

Uppsala
January 1982

E.J.S.

One

Theology and 'Religious Studies'

Among all the subjects which appear in the curricula of western educational institutions, none seem to be more difficult to explain to outsiders than those connected with religion. It matters little under what names they appear in the handbooks – 'divinity', 'theology', 'comparative religion' and 'religious studies' are all options – few who have not taken part in them (and not all those who have) seem to know quite what they are supposed to achieve. Even highly qualified academics in other fields seem often to be as nonplussed as the rawest first-year student when it comes to fitting these courses into the pattern of (particularly) higher education. All too often it seems to be assumed that the study of religion can have only one purpose, namely, the deepening of personal religious belief; those who make this assumption will, however, often proceed to argue that religious belief is such an intensely personal affair that it is improper to admit anything connected with it into an academic community committed to other standards entirely. Faith (it is argued) is not the same thing as knowledge. Indeed, it may be the very opposite of knowledge. And if this is so, then surely it cannot have any place in a modern community of learning. If and when it does appear, it tends to be assumed either that it is a survival from a more or less remote academic past or that its only *raison d'être* has to do with the training of men and women for full-time religious professions.

A further element in this particular cluster of assumptions is that since most modern western universities (it is with universities that we are mainly concerned) are 'secular', and since 'secular' normally means 'separated from the sphere of religious influence', therefore the teaching of religion can have no place in their everyday activities. On the principle of free association, students may of course be permitted to hold religious meetings, but the university, if it is to remain true to its secular nature, ought not to offer teaching in this disputed area. Churches and other religious organisations may do what they please in whatever educational institutions they may happen to control, provided that they do not expect public money to be contributed to their upkeep. But to the extent to which the state – any state – either holds itself aloof from all religion or declines to support one group of believers over against another, it cannot be expected to finance the teaching of religion. This principle has been fairly rigidly adhered to in the United States of America; elsewhere various compromises have been arrived at, depending on the power of the churches and the demands of *Realpolitik*. But on the whole the principle obtains, that religion is either kept at arm's length from higher education or, where it has been admitted, it has been as a Cinderella subject. Or, as Ninian Smart once put it, having lost the place it once occupied as the Queen of Sciences, it has been forced into the role of the Knave of Arts.

Behind higher education there is of course primary and secondary education. And in many western countries (though the United States again is an exception), religion is taught in schools, often on a compulsory but non-examinable basis. In my school the subject was called 'divinity', though again there are alternatives, 'Religious Education', 'Religious Instruction' or whatever. But the overall pattern is depressingly familiar. For complex reasons, which I do not propose to discuss in detail here, it is all too often taught ineffectively by ill-prepared teachers (or the local minister) to unwilling pupils. Some years ago, the late Monsignor Ronald Knox described a phenomenon which he called 'public-school [i.e. private school] religion' in these waspish terms:

> ... public schools are trying to teach the sons of gentlemen a religion in which their mothers believe, and their fathers would like to: a religion without 'enthusiasm' in the old sense, reserved in its self-expression, calculated to reinforce morality, chivalry, and the sense of truth, providing comfort in times of distress and a glow of contentment in declining years; supernatural in its nominal doctrines, yet on the whole rationalistic in its mode of approaching God: tolerant of other people's tenets, yet sincere about its own, regular in church-going, generous to charities, ready to put up with the defects of the local clergyman. This

religion the schoolmaster is under contract to teach ... (Knox, 1950: 17).

Knox's public schoolmaster was 'under contract' to teach religion, and religion in that case was Anglican Christianity, watered down in a generally moralising direction. The broad outline is all too recognisable – a type of moral education, supported by 'Bible stories' and by ill-digested gobbets of ancient history, but pointed in the direction of good citizenship and safe membership in a not-too-demanding church. The first of these goals is sometimes achieved (though more usually for reasons unconnected with the schools' religious instruction); the latter seldom. The intention of the teaching of religion in schools, in short, has generally been to reinforce the churches, and especially the established church of the land. Increasingly it has failed to do so. But it is perhaps not surprising that when the study of religion emerges on a higher rung of the educational ladder it should be regarded as an extension of substantially the same activity. After all, university physics builds on school physics, university geography on school geography, university music on school music; is it not reasonable to suppose that university study of religion will be built on foundations laid in school?

It is here that we stand at the parting of the ways between divinity/theology and religious studies. For while theology (or divinity) proceeds along a path not essentially dissimilar to that generally followed in secondary schools, religious studies does something rather different. It is in respect of theology that radicals question the right of the subject to a place in the secular academic sun. For as a rule they too have experienced an older type of religious education in schools, and fail to see how that kind of exercise could be justified on the university level. The trouble is, that they are often unaware of any viable alternative approach.

In the remainder of this chapter I shall consider some of the differences between theology and religious studies, partly in respect of their subject matter, and partly in respect of the attitude of mind they require on the student's part.

*

There has probably never been a religious tradition in any part of the world which has not made provisions for the teaching of its own deepest insights, and for the continuation of its sacred organisation. All have made demands in respect of mental discipline and intellectual, as well as spiritual, application. In primal societies, those traditions of the family or tribe which relate to the powerful world of the spirits and the ancestors have to be learned, as have the times and seasons and correct ways in which rituals must be carried out, if the well-being of the people is to be secured. Men must learn the men's rituals: women the women's rituals. Initiation into the full rank and privileges of adulthood will be preceded by a period of training under the guidance of elders; perhaps, too, by a period of solitude and bodily deprivation in quest of a personal 'guardian spirit'. Nothing will be left to chance, and there will be very little room for free improvisation. Once a certain stage of cultural formation has been passed, myth, story and legend will be learned with precision, in order that they may be passed on unaltered to coming generations. To fail to play one's part in the chain of sacred tradition is certainly possible; but in pre-secular societies it is uncommon.

In archaic societies and cultures, particular demands are made of those specialists in the life of the spirit whom we normally designate by the term *shaman*. Pricisely what constitutes a shaman is not easy to say in a few words, though his or her chief function is to cure illness and to prevent death caused by spirit activity. In general, the shaman is a people's main means of communication with the world of the all-powerful spirits; and though he may have some inborn aptitude for this role (for instance, in his ability to enter into trance-states), effective commerce with the spirits is something which he must learn, and for which he must be trained. To this end, he must be chosen, and must place himself under the guidance of either a living shaman or the ghost of a dead one, through dreams and visions.

The effort is not a purely intellectual one, but rather an act of total submission, a death of the normally conscious self, without which he simply cannot function. Put in the strongest possible terms, 'a man must die before he becomes a shaman.' There is however an intellectual element involved in the learning process, since the shaman, as well as learning ecstatic techniques, must consciously learn to identify spirits, to interpret myths, to manipulate a secret language and to use items of equipment. But all these things take place strictly within the sacred traditions of the people to whom he belongs, and whose spiritual servant he is called to be.

This same motive – of placing oneself under spiritual discipline in order to gain a particular insight into the innermost nature of things – runs like a scarlet thread through the history of religions. It is especially marked in Indian religion, where the deepest knowledge of Reality is always assumed to be passed down along a chain of tradition, from master (*guru*) to pupil (*shishya, chela*).

> This highest mystery of the Veda's end
> Was propounded in an earlier age;
> Let it not be taught to an unquiet man,
> Or to one who is neither son nor pupil.
>
> To the great-souled man who loyally
> And greatly loves [his] God,
> Who loves his spiritual master even as his God,
> The matter of this discourse will shine with clearest light, –
> With clearest light will shine.
>
> (Zaehner, 1966: 217)

In Hindu and Buddhist traditions alike, the heart of metaphysical teaching is expressed in dialogue form – not the Socratic dialogue in which a skilful teacher teases out of an astounded pupil matter which the pupil never imagined that he knew, but the respectful dialogue of the ignorant pupil and the wise *guru*. In the Chhandogya Upanishad, for instance, Narada comes to Sanatkumara, saying, 'Teach me, sir.' 'What do you know?' the *guru* asks, and when he hears that the pupil knows all the traditions without having discerned their innermost meaning, he proceeds to unfold, step by step, the nature of the Self (*atman*). The pupil does not only have to want to know; he has to trust implicitly that what he is being told is the truth, and that involves his placing unquestioning trust in the spiritual integrity and attainments of the *guru*. This is the quality of 'faith' (*śraddha*), trust and submission in the face of superior wisdom. Says Sanatkumara: 'When one has faith, then one thinks. No one thinks until he has faith. Only by having faith does one think. So [you] should really want to understand faith.' To this, Narada replies: 'Sir, I really do want to understand faith' (Zaehner, 1966: 112-20).

This 'teaching in depth' is not to be disseminated at random, but only from a trustworthy teacher to a trusted pupil.' "Artabhaga, my friend," said he [Yajñavalkya], "take my hand. We two alone will know about this. It is not for us [to speak of this] in public." Together they went away and conversed together ...' (Zaehner, 1966: 50).

The same principle, of intimate, person-to-person teaching on a basis of implicit faith, is carried over into the monastic life, though with the obvious difference that some, at least, of the teaching is passed on in classes rather than individually. Even though some monasteries in both eastern and western countries became veritable universities, capable of accommodating thousands of students, still each student would have a personal *guru* or spiritual director from whose hands, finally, he would accept initiation. This same principle is present in the Judaeo-Christian tradition from a very early stage. The *Rule* of the Qumran Community states that the Master

> ... shall admit into the Covenant of Grace all those who have freely devoted themselves to the observance of God's precepts, that they may be joined to the counsel of God and may live perfectly before Him in accordance with all that has been revealed concerning their appointed times ... [Those who enter the community] shall bring all their knowledge, powers, and possessions into the Community of God, that they may purify their knowledge in the truth of God's precepts and order their powers according to His ways of perfection ... (Vermes, 1962:72).

We may compare the mediaeval Christian monk, who acquired his religious formation '... individually, under the guidance of an abbot, a spiritual father, through the reading of the Bible and the Fathers, within the liturgical framework of the monastic life' (Leclerq, 1962:13).

No matter where we seek in the religious literature of the presecular world, we shall find the same principle emerging: that true knowledge of what is most important and most real in religion is never granted to the casual and seldom to the solitary student, but comes only as a result of total dedication to the life of study, an unquestioning acceptance of spiritual guidance. Certainly there may come a time in the life of the individual when he has learned all his spiritual director has to teach, after which he will be 'on his own' as a hermit, *sannyasin* or *sadhu*; but this is always seen as the ultimate quest, and not as a point of departure.

The implication is that the true life of study will inevitably mean separation from the corrosive influences of an outside world which is either morally corrupt or ontologically 'unreal'. Not that God is altogether absent from that world; but total knowledge comes only from total dedication, being found only within the community whose life is based on what God (or the Real) has shown to the dedicated.

Basically, therefore, the 'study of religion' in the presecular world involves total trust on the student's part in either (a) the integrity of a community and its spiritual values, (b) the normative quality of a particular chain of divine revelation, and hence its 'truth' – whether that revelation be embodied in sacred scripture or in a sacred tradition of interpretation, or (c) the personal spiritual credentials of a particular teacher, or *guru*, virtually irrespective of what he or she actually teaches. In the first of these cases, emphasis will characteristically be placed on the social function of commerce with the unseen world (the healing of disease, the achievement of good hunting, contact with the spirits of the departed); in the second, the major stress will be on the conceptual content of what is revealed, on verbalisation and minutely correct ritual performance; in the third case, personal dependence on the teacher and on the community over which he presides will take precedence over all else. The teacher becomes a father-surrogate and the community a substitute family, within which the devotee is relieved of final personal responsibility on condition that he or she learns and observes the doctrines and conventions which obtain within the group: often indeed a sect will call itself a 'family' and style its head as 'father' or 'mother'.

But in every case to 'study religion' is to study only what the community and its representatives, or an individual teacher, are prepared to attest as being worthy of study: a particular Scripture or group of scriptures; the interpretations previously put forward by authoritative teachers, sometimes against the background of 'false teachings' against which an individual or a community have rebelled in the past; and the detailed mode of life which the community has accepted as its own, involving conventions about dress, food, livelihood, language, worship and social behaviour generally. The assumption is always that the tradition in question enshrines all that the individual *needs* to know; and sometimes that it contains all that he or she *ought* to know, since whatever lies outside the authoritative revelation is at best irrelevant, and at worst positively dangerous.

It was substantially this pattern of study which dominated the universities of the Christian West down to approximately the end of the nineteenth century. It was expected that those studying religion would be Christians, members of a particular denomination and preparing themselves for the work of the Christian ministry or priesthood. They would therefore already have accepted the credal basis of their church, and therefore also its authority in all matters pertaining to faith. To be sure, a degree of questioning was permitted within certain limits, and by the end of the nineteenth century critical scholarship had advanced far enough to enable much theological study to be carried on in accordance with 'scientific' standards – more especially in respect of philological and historical accuracy. Indeed, so powerful was the late nineteenth-century emphasis on history as the medium within which God had (so it was believed) chosen to reveal himself, that the impression was created that the study of theology was mainly a matter of the study of the history of the old Israel and the new, a history which did not even need to be explained to make its impression. (It is the debased form of this unwarranted assumption which has in the course of time led to at least some of the inefficient teaching of religion which I mentioned at the beginning of this chapter.)

Theological syllabuses have for almost a century been consistent both in what they do, and what they do not, teach. As far back as 1915, the theologian P.T. Forsyth wrote that, in fact, '... the study of theology (in so far as it transcends a philosophy of natural religion or a spiritual anthropology) means either the science of the Bible, or the science of revelation, or the science of the Church's mind – the study of Christian origins, of the Christian message, and of the Christian society made by that message and explicating it by work and thought in relation to natural society' (Forsyth, 1915: 299 f.). Although these words were written almost three-quarters of a century ago, they are still broadly applicable in the 1980s, as even a cursory examination of present-day Christian theological syllabuses shows. Their terminology varies, but their content centres on four areas of study. First comes the study of the Old Testament, as far as possible in the original Hebrew. Secondly there is the study of the New Testament, again as far as possible in the original Greek (though since Greek is generally considered to be an easier language than Hebrew, the linguistic content is higher in respect of the New

Testament than of the Old). The third area is Ecclesiastical History, with a particular emphasis on the developments of the early Christian centuries, and in Protestant institutions, on the sixteenth-century Reformation. And the fourth, which may have various names, centres on the study of Western philosophy and theology, separately and in interaction.

Other subjects may from time to time be added to it – for instance 'comparative religion' – but the quartet of Old and New Testaments, with their attendant Hebrew and Greek, ecclesiastical history and 'philosophical theology' is almost always there. Clearly it has come to be assumed that in this core syllabus there is to be found everything, or practically everything, which the serious western student *must* know about religion, either for the purpose of entry into full-time Christian work or at least in order to gain an intelligent understanding of the place of religion in the western world.

This is perhaps not the place to enter into a detailed discussion of whether this assumption is a correct one. That would carry us far outside the bounds of this investigation. But three critical points may be made. The first is that this approach to the Christian material is extremely selective, and makes little or no effort to deal with even the Christian tradition as a whole, being concerned mainly to pass from landmark to landmark without giving a great deal of thought to who set up the landmarks in the first place, or what kind of country lies between them. The second is that it is one-sidedly historical, and leaves practically no room for what 'religious studies' regards as of prime importance, namely the varied *functions* of religion in the lives of individuals and communities. And thirdly, the 'core syllabus', since it generally succeeds in omitting almost everything that is characteristic of the religious life of the present day, inadvertently conveys the impression that that life is either unimportant, or at least unsuitable for high-level academic study.

Fortunately, more and more attempts are being made in these days to escape from this syllabus in its more rigid forms. In far too many cases, however, the only way in which this can be done is to introduce supplementary 'electives' or 'options' – always under the understanding that these must not be allowed to interfere with the serious study of the Bible and the other traditional subjects. These additional courses may be extremely varied, depending on the interests and capabilities of whoever happens to be on a particular teaching staff at a particular time; but they are seldom regarded as being other than peripheral to the main object of the exercise, which is to communicate knowledge of the essentials of the Christian tradition.

Those involved in the teaching of theology along these lines are often either incomprehending, or resentful, if asked to justify the content of their syllabus. *Of course* the Bible has to be taught in the original languages; *of course* we must know (though not necessarily understand) what happened to the Christian Church during its first four formative centuries; *of course* Kant, Hegel, Hume and Schleiermacher are important. Why should we ask these impertinent questions? The tradition is self-justifying, and if things are left out they are unimportant, and deserve to be left out. Other subjects and approaches can be added to the syllabus, provided that nothing is done to disturb the fundamentals.

Now it is no part of my present purpose to suggest that the traditional Christian subjects have no place in a course of study designed to prepare men and women for a fuller understanding of the Christian tradition. But I do suggest that their place is not to be justified on the grounds that 'we have always done it this way', or that their rights are self-evident.

*

Over against 'theology' there is in these days a subject which most people by now have come to call 'religious studies'. It has inherited some of the attitudes and approaches of what was once called 'comparative religion', without being identical with it. But it is similar, in that it is prepared to attempt to study religion, not on a basis of one tradition (or a part of a tradition) only, but 'in the round'. Of course it accepts limitations: total knowledge of all the world's religions is a stark impossibility in one lifetime. But its limitations are imposed upon it from within, in the competence and capabilities of those who teach the subject, and not from without, in what may have traditionally been regarded as authoritative, normative, suitable or desirable for the student to spend his time doing.

A typical 'religious studies' syllabus will contain historical, thematic and methodological courses. There will be broad survey courses covering some of the great religious traditions of the world in their historical development and their doctrines and forms of expression: Hinduism, Buddhism, Islam will take their place alongside the Judaeo-Christian tradition as expressions of the religious life of mankind; so too will 'primal', minority and 'alternative' forms of religious belief and practice. Thematic studies presuppose a certain degree of familiarity on the student's part with the historically factual material, and concern themselves with, for instance, myth, ritual, architecture, iconography, social expressions, ethics and the like, bringing together more than one local form in the interests of a better overall understanding of the ways in which religion expresses itself in human life. The 'methodological' courses, finally, will explore the various ways in which religion is capable of being studied, the approaches which may be brought to bear upon the subject matter, and their history in the context of Western (and other) ideas.

It is sometimes claimed that there is no significant difference between the respective approaches of theology and religious studies, the two being separated not by method, but only by the material to which they are prepared to address themselves. But on this point it is hard to generalise. As a rule, educationally speaking, 'theology' in western cultures implies 'Christian theology' (though there are of course Jewish, Muslim and Hindu theologies as well). And in traditional Christian terms, the starting point of theology has always been held to be belief in God, or rather the *fact* of God, who has made himself known in revelation and to whom believers respond. But this is only a point of departure. Technically, the theological student works in virtually the same way as the religious studies specialist: he is equally concerned with causes and effects, with the interplay of faith and beliefs, institutional forms and ethical precepts. He may well claim that by remaining more or less strictly within one religious tradition, he can achieve a deeper and more genuine grasp of cardinal issues than that which is accessible to the world traveller or the cosmic visionary, who may so easily degenerate into a dilettante.

But there is little consensus these days as to what precisely constitutes a theologian. In the late 1960s, an American scholar wrote that '[t]he happenings to which the theologian directs his hearers are believed to represent, and even to disclose, in some positive and decisive way ultimate truth or reality' (Eckardt, 1968: xxv). But at least the theologian looks at *happenings*. And it is surely possible to ask, 'Believed by whom?' By the theologian himself, or only by the community of believers to whom his studies are directed? On this point it is again not possible to generalise, particularly where modern secular culture is concerned. The mere fact of being, or claiming to be, a theologian, is not necessarily the same thing as being, or claiming to be, a believer. Indeed, one of the great problems facing theology in the modern secular world is that of justifying the study of that in which one no longer believes, and of serving a community of which one no longer feels oneself to be a member.

It may be no more than a sign of the times, but a remarkable number of Christian theologians (professionally so-called) have in recent years felt impelled to move away from the straightforward and well-defined study of the contents of the Christian tradition into the wider field of religious studies. We may mention the names of Tillich, Hick, Davis, Cox and Robinson as examples of this 'widening' process. Each was forced to accept, after many years of 'traditional' Christian studies, that its methods were unsatisfactory to answer the questions posed by the phenomenon of religion in the modern world. I am not aware of any similar movement away from religious studies into the narrower field of traditional Christian theology.

To be sure, the broadening process is not without its dangers. In leaving behind a single well-defined area of study one may land, willy-nilly, in an uncharted desert. There have been, and are, teachers and students of religious studies whose generalisations bear little relation to the facts of the case in any of the specific areas dealt with, and who are rather apt to claim expertise on the basis of the cursory reading of one or two second-hand sources. These the theologian may well quote in support of his case, and urge that close linguistic study of the Judaeo-Christian sources serves to protect the student against such excesses of enthusiasm. And so it may, in certain cases. But it will not do to compare theology at its best with religious studies at its worst. Either may be badly taught and mechanically followed, and there is little point in trying to escape from the caricature of one by embracing the caricature of the other.

It must be admitted that, at its best, theology can offer a depth of understanding of one tradition which must remain inaccessible to the generalist. At its best, religious studies can reveal the principles on which all religious belief and behaviour rests, when viewed from the angle of the believer – principles which once grasped, can be applied in every separate area. At the gate of traditional Christian theology there stands the motto: 'Believe in order to understand.' Religious studies has no such rubric, merely the expectation that the student will take absolutely seriously the right of the believer, of whatever tradition, country, or period, to hold certain beliefs about the nature of the world he lives in, and to act in accordance with those beliefs. Many years ago now, the Norwegian scholar W. Brede Kristensen wrote that as far as the student is concerned, 'there exists no other religious reality [that is, nothing which the student is capable of observing] than the faith of the believer' (Kristensen, 1954: 27). To enter into the discipline of religious studies is therefore to accept that faith for what it claims to be, namely a window on to the unseen world of the powers which control men's destinies and a map of the seen and the unseen universe. Whether or not that map is an adequate one according to the student's own inherited understanding is of no consequence; what is important is that the student should accept it as coherent and indeed inevitable, given the premises on which it is based.

Shortly we shall have the opportunity to inquire more fully into the very real dilemma in which the student is placed who, being fully committed to one religious tradition, attempts to enter with some degree of sympathy into the innermost sanctuary of another. For the moment, it will be enough to acknowledge that the difficulty is there, and that there are perhaps very few students who are not troubled by it at some time or other. To be sure, the student of theology may in some circumstances be more or less immune from the troubles of the divided mind: remaining within the tradition which he has come to call his own, and taught along orthodox lines by elder brethren from within the company of believers, whatever his troubles may be, they do not commonly involve conflicting religious loyalties. Within religious studies, on the other hand, the sensitive student cannot always keep the material at arm's length. Indeed, the greater his sensitivity the more likely it is that what begins as a quest for intellectual understanding will gradually transmute itself into a matter of imperious spiritual necessity.

Is it not then 'safer' for the student to be guided first of all into a closer and deeper understanding of those forms of religion which have exercised the greatest influence on the culture of which he is part? And ought he not to be dissuaded from widening his horizons until he has, so to speak, made himself a citizen of his own country? The argument has often been put forward that, in Ronald Knox's celebrated epigram, 'Comparative religion [i.e. the study of religions other than Christianity] is an admirable recipe for making people comparatively religious' (Knox, 1952: 105). And since it is man's destiny to be *absolutely* religious within a divinely ordained system of truth and falsehood, to follow 'gods many and lords many', though perhaps justifiable at the bar of intellect, is a sure path to spiritual suicide.

To argue in these terms is, however, to make certain assumptions about the kind of world in which we live, and about the way in which it is governed. It assumes, first, that as far as the western student is concerned, the culture of which he is part, in so far as it has a religious component at all, acknowledges only Judaism and Christianity as adequate to fill that role. Even if this were so (and today it is a very questionable assumption), to arrive at an overall understanding of the roles of Judaism and Christianity in Western culture would make very great demands of the student. It is all very well to argue that because the *origins* of Christianity are being examined in some detail, the tradition *as a whole* is being mastered. It is not. Conventional theological syllabuses in fact omit almost everything that is distinctive of twentieth-century (as opposed to first-, fourth- or sixteenth-century) Christianity. They communicate a great deal about the *content* of the Bible, but pay scant attention to the *function* of the Bible in the life of faith. They go through some periods in the life of the Church with a fine-tooth comb; others they leave almost entirely untouched. They pay practically no attention to the arts – music, painting, architecture, sculpture and the rest. They seem to be unaware that Christianity has a long history, and independent traditions of thought, in Africa, Asia, Latin America and many other parts of the world far distant from the North Atlantic axis. They shy away from spirituality and 'mysticism', and may perhaps have helped to turn many young people to exotic spiritualities simply because they have failed to tell those same young people that there are discoveries to be made much nearer home than India and Tibet. For the lives of ordinary Christians, their places and times of worship, their festivals and pilgrimages, their rites of passage, their psalms and hymns and spiritual songs, their hopes and fears and enthusiasms, the traditional 'agreed syllabus' demonstrates unconcern amounting almost to contempt.

For the developments of the last quarter-century (which is after all the period which has shaped the minds of those who fondly believe themselves to be 'contemporary'), the syllabus has almost no time at all.

While on this subject, a final question may be asked. Why, in the matter of recent Christian thought, should it be assumed that almost the only modern theologians worthy of the name are all Germans? This is perhaps not such a new idea, and in one way or another it has left its mark on generations of theological students (probably ever since the days of Goethe). All the same, it is a questionable assumption. German theology is written in a language which practically no English-speaking student has even begun to study, and has to be placed against a cultural and political background far different from that of Britain, North America and Australasia. I would not for a moment wish to suggest that it is either unimportant or insignificant. But where it is taught, it is all too often taught superficially, and I question in any case whether it should be regarded as normative, particularly when it leads the English-speaking student to ignore and undervalue home-grown products. Let the theologian study Barth, Brunner, Bultmann and Bonhoeffer, Moltmann, Tillich and Käsemann by all means. But have Maurice, Forsyth, John and Donald Baillie, Temple, Ramsey, Oman, Quick and Farmer nothing to teach him? And how often do any of these figure in conventional theological syllabuses?

*

Even if it were true that Christianity enjoyed a position of undisputed supremacy in the western world, there would be every reason to ask serious questions about the way in which theology is taught in its educational institutions. In fact Christianity no longer occupies any such position. Of course, the Christian churches collectively still have great numerical strength in Western countries. But in a period of vast international mobility and interdependence, in which an Islamic revival in Iran can have an immediate and devastating effect on workers in Detroit or Birmingham, and in which the Pope and the Archbishop of Canterbury are in some Western circles less well regarded than the Dalai Lama, the Maharishi Mahesh Yogi and His Divine Grace A.C. Bhaktivedanta

Swami Prabhupada, there would appear to be pressing reasons why even the Western student should sit up and take notice. And this involves rather more than the attempt to assemble, on the basis of an authority which most no longer acknowledge, 'proofs' that Islam, Tibetan Buddhism, or the Hindu *bhakti* tradition are unworthy of serious consideration. For an increasing number of Westerners – not least young people –it is Christianity which is no longer taken seriously, for a variety of reasons which the Christian community as a whole has so far shown very little desire fully to investigate, and which theology as presently constituted has very little chance of investigating.

But the basic difficulty remains, that while theology is normally able to presuppose that students hold a secure place *within* the tradition being studied, religious studies is able to assume only that the student wishes to grasp something of the role of religion as an aspect of human life, and is prepared in pursuit of this quest to turn to cultural areas remote from his own. Direct first-hand experience has to be replaced by something far less quantifiable – by the exercise of imaginative sympathy. This, it is sometimes argued, is to abandon the relative security of one's spiritual homeland for the dangers of the uncharted seas. At least, it may be argued, no student should be encouraged to move out into the wide world of the religions until he has become thoroughly familiar with the tradition in which he belongs, and which has done so much to shape his own culture.

In our next chapter we shall examine the question of commitment as the royal road to intellectual understanding. But first, two small but important observations.

First, it cannot have escaped the notice of today's educationalists that very many students no longer acknowledge the Judaeo-Christian tradition as a positive element in western society. To demand of a student who is emotionally alienated from that tradition that it must be studied before anything else in the world of religion, is apt to be received more as an unwarranted authoritarian imposition than as the gift of the keys of the kingdom.

And secondly, even the study of the Judaeo-Christian past does not absolve the student from the exercise of imaginative sympathy. When ordinary Christian students find it almost impossible to enter imaginatively into the Christianity of a hundred years ago, which they dismiss with a phrase such as 'Victorian smugness' or 'imperialistic arrogance', and decline to study more closely, is it not likely that the same difficulty will present itself magnified a thousandfold when the time comes to examine Christian origins or the Protestant Reformation? One suspects in both these cases that what is being studied is less the first or the sixteenth century than the impression which each has left on the mind of the twentieth. And that the personal qualities on which religious studies tries to insist are, in such cases as these, mainly conspicuous by their absence.

But having made these two points, it is time to take a further step, and consider the question of how the student's religious commitment (or the absence of it) might be related to the study of religion.

Two

Commitment and Understanding

We have seen that there are broadly speaking two ways of 'studying' religion, one from a position within, and the other from a position outside the community of those whose lives are shaped by religious beliefs and practices. Insiders are often seeking to make more firm their grasp of the tradition to which they belong, while the others – a mixture of insiders, outsiders and don't-knows – are looking for intellectual explanations of what, in human terms, it is to be religious.

Now we must ask whether what we in the West generally call 'religious commitment' is a help or a hindrance along this second path, the path of 'religious studies'.

But before we proceed to discuss the question in the terms in which we have raised it, a word of warning will be necessary. 'Commitment' is a concept which strictly speaking belongs within the orbit of fairly recent Protestant Christianity, and cannot without more ado be transferred to other religio-cultural areas. It makes no sense at all to talk about commitment unless there is a real possibility of being uncommitted, that is, unless there is a strong element of free choice involved in the individual's religion. Where religion is co-extensive with a social order (as in primal societies, in much of Judaism, Hinduism and Islam), then the free choice element is slight or non-existent. One may of course observe religious precepts and practices with greater or less regularity, intensity and enthusiasm; but seldom is there greater or less 'commitment' in the sense in which the Protestant Christian – whose religion is almost always in the last resort a matter of free choice and free association – understands the word.

Nowhere, however, is the impact of Protestant Christianity on the religious mind of the West more clearly seen than in the practically unquestioned assumption that 'genuine' religion is a matter of personal convictions arrived at individually. And since this is certainly the way in which most students begin to tackle these questions, we shall on this occasion accept its practical legitimacy as an angle of approach, while insisting that it is only one among many.

'Understanding', too, is a problematical term, mainly because of its built-in element of subjectivity. But again, it is so much taken for granted that the aim of the student of religion is to 'understand' religious phenomena, that is, to gain an informed and intuitive grasp of the conditions governing religious belief and practice on a world map, that we shall use it here without further attempt to define precisely what it might, and might not, mean. Perhaps 'explanation' would be a less controversial term than 'understanding', though again our aim on this occasion is to consider a controversial question more or less in the terms in which that question is commonly asked.

Having made these preliminary points, we may perhaps begin by constructing an imaginary debate between the representatives of two positions, one claiming that 'commitment' is a help to the student of religion, the other urging that it is a hindrance.

*

On one wing of the debate there are those who use an argument which goes something like this: to be 'religiously committed' is to stand in a definite personal relationship to the unseen world which is believed to control human destiny. This relationship is one of dependence, and involves attitudes of the mind and the will, as well as of the emotions. Because the one who is committed in this way has experienced in his own life what the outsider can only ever view from a distance, he can grasp intuitively what the religious experience means to others beside himself: he knows the force of the religious imperative at first hand, with all its hopes and fears, ecstasies and disappointments, and above all the way in which it relativises all purely human concerns. Surely, therefore, there can be no doubt about the matter: the believer knows something which the agnostic or the atheist can never know. The agnostic and the atheist can observe and evaluate the outward machinery of religion, but what they cannot do is to grasp the divine-human relationship which lies at its heart.

Very often this argument has been bolstered by the analogy of music. Music cannot be 'understood' unless it can first be heard. Those who are unable to hear or those who refuse to listen can observe the mechanics of music: they can see mouths opening and closing, fingers moving, instruments being blown, beaten, plucked and scraped, and they can describe precisely what they see. But because they cannot hear the notes, they are unable even to begin to sense the chain of communication which passes from composer, through performer, to listener. Religion, the argument concludes, is similar. It involves, behind all its trivial observables, a communication, and only those who have ears to hear, can know what it is. Commitment is the capacity to hear and the will to listen. Therefore it can never be a barrier to understanding; on the contrary, it is the one condition which makes understanding possible.

Were the analogy a perfect one, the argument would be unanswerable. But this the uncommitted will not accept. He brushes the musical argument aside, pointing out that it appeals, not to the reason but only to the imagination. It would only work, he points out, if the believer knew *beyond any shadow of a doubt* that religion actually refers itself to a supernatural or a transcendent order, and were capable of demonstrating its control over the universe on the one hand, and its communication with the world on the other. This he cannot do. He has never been able to do so, and he will never be able to do so. Otherwise, what he calls his 'faith' or his 'experience' may spoil his understanding, by persuading him to waste valuable time speculating on the source of religious phenomena, instead of looking long and hard at the phenomena themselves. They may have other causes. And if faith leads one to miss things like the impact on religion of politics, economics, environment, culture, group behaviour and a great many other things, then it has not helped the believer to understand religious phenomena: rather the reverse, since it persuades him to reduce complex human relationships to an attractive but over-simplified matter of a one-to-one relationship between man and the supernatural.

But that is still not all. Look at the actual record of religious believers, the sceptic urges. Can it be denied that powerful (and no doubt sincere, though mistaken) commitment to one religious position has usually led those involved, not to appreciate, but to pour scorn upon, what they evidently regard as the false or mistaken commitment of others? One might well suspect that the stronger the commitment of an individual or a community to one set of religious values (which the believer claims to be so helpful when it comes to understanding all the others), the *less* likely they are to give much thought to what other people may believe; and if they do notice these alternative values, as a rule they do so only to call them in question or condemn them. Whatever mutual understanding there may be comes about, not when religious traditions are strong and powerful, but when they are weak and in search of allies.

One last sceptical point. Who could seriously claim (it is asked) that deeply committed believers are the best interpreters of their own tradition? Surely all the evidence points in the opposite direction – that the deeper a person's commitment, the more likely he is to accept any cock-and-bull story that happens to be going the rounds, provided that it strengthens the cause he believes in. Believers are not the only offenders; if anything, the political *canaille* is even worse. In both cases, emotional commitment to a cause puts blinkers on whoever happens to get caught up in it. He can understand nothing properly – neither that in which he *is* involved nor that in which he is *not* involved. To take a biblical illustration, as long as the Prophet Jonah was inside his 'great fish' he understood nothing of either his fish or any other fish in the sea, though he remembered to say his prayers to his God. Only after the fish had spat him out on to dry land again did the experience begin to make sense to him.

From this imaginary debate, three alternatives emerge in the matter of commitment and understanding. The first is the claim that because of his commitment, the believer has a vast advantage when it comes to an instinctive understanding of religion. The second is the opposite claim that commitment is a barrier to understanding because it tends to prevent individuals from seeing religion in any other perspective than their own. The third claim is that commitment can give valuable insights into the religious life *once it has been left behind* and the individual has returned to the safety of dry land.

Let us now consider these three alternatives in a little more detail, taking them in reverse order.

Past commitment

Although one ought not to conclude that 'the only good commitment is a dead commitment,' the progression from the more intense type of religious involvement to a life of scholarship is not an uncommon one. A former teacher of mine, the late Professor S.G.F. Brandon of Manchester, used to say that his understanding of especially the ritual aspect of religion had been immeasurably helped by his training and experience as an Anglo-Catholic priest. Because of his past experience he knew what if felt like to wear sacred vestments, to stand at an altar, to ring bells, to swing a thurible and to carry out 'the sacrifice of the Mass'. He was no longer an active priest; but without this experience, on his own testimony his understanding (and hence his scholarship) would have been immeasurably the poorer.

This is one example I happen to know about. Scholars are not always so forthcoming in the matter of what they may once have experienced, but have in the course of time outgrown as part of their normal and natural development. Scholars are not born; they are made; and in their younger days often learned from contacts which they afterward left behind. The Swedish Islamist and psychologist of religion Tor Andrae, for instance, once wrote of his experiences in a Swedish country vicarage in the late nineteenth century, where he learned not only the basics of Christianity (from his father), but also the folklore of the district (from the servants). Another Swedish scholar of a former generation, Nathan Söderblom, absorbed the Swedish Lutheran pietism of his native province and the American revivalism of Dwight Moody before taking his doctorate at the Sorbonne. In my own case (if I may be permitted to join such august company) I am happy to acknowledge all that I was taught by the Methodists of North Lancashire and County Durham in my late teens and early twenties: because I have sat among them in their pews, and even stood as a Local Preacher in their pulpits – because I was in fact one of them – I believe that I know things about everyday religious life which I otherwise could never have learned. The stream of life has carried me beyond them, and perhaps today they would hardly recognise me. But my debt of gratitude is none the less real for all that. If pressed, I would have to admit that I can no longer affirm everything in the area of religion which I was able to affirm in those days, and in that sense mine, too, is a case of 'past commitment'. But one cannot safely repudiate one's personal history, and I tend to feel just a little sorry for those students of religion (some of them in very exalted positions) who appear either to have had no comparable exposure to its everyday life, or having had it, wish that they had not.

For the experience of past commitment can work in precisely the opposite way, if, that is, it be classified among the 'childish things' which, having been outgrown, are regarded as best forgotten. In such cases, a break with religion can result in an intense feeling of antagonism both toward the individual's rejected past, and toward all those who still persist in treading the old paths. This does not prevent further study; it is, however, likely to dictate the goal toward which study is aimed, often the exposure of the fallacies of religion and the weakness of those human beings who still persist in taking it seriously. A good example of this would be the American psychologist of religion James H. Leuba earlier this century, who had a Salvation Army 'conversion experience' in his youth, apparently regretted it profoundly, and spent his working life trying to explain away everything which it might have involved. He believed himself, in a manner of speaking, to have emerged from the darkness of religion into the light of reason, and like many another rationalist and quondam believer, felt that he was a better and more impartial scholar for having put personal religion firmly behind him.

But feelings of guilt and shame over past weaknesses interpret little and distort much. Where past religious commitment is utterly rejected, it may at a later stage produce feelings similar to those with which the cured alcoholic passes the door of a public house which he dare not trust himself to enter. Religion in these terms all too easily becomes a weakness, if not a disease (perhaps, as Freud believed, a neurosis); and though one may still study the symptoms in others, one must avoid the risk of fresh infection.

Of course, what many younger students of religion claim to have rejected is not really commitment at all, but superficial contact with some of the outward forms of religion, coupled with some very vague second or third-hand impressions drawn from a variety of sources. The literature of today's 'alternative religions', for instance, is full of bitter criticisms of 'establishment religion', most of which convey the impression that the critics are prepared to accept anyone's opinion about the character of the religious mainstream, provided that it fits their generally negative view of western society. I mention this not to add to my argument, but merely to suggest that superficial outside impressions are not to be equated without more ado with the 'past commitment' that we are discussing.

We may perhaps sum up by saying that there is a sense in which past commitment can be extremely valuable to the student, but that its value depends on whether or not it is integrated into the later life of the individual concerned. Where it is not – where it is rejected emotionally with a sense of shame or guilt or outrage, anything which it might have contained (or which is capable of being compared with it) is almost bound to be seen in a distorted perspective.

No religious commitment

If by 'religious commitment' we mean the fully conscious acceptance of a scale of values established by tradition within a particular community of believers, then one must conclude that everything will depend on what those values are, and what they involve. It need scarcely be said that they are not identical in every case, and that wide variations are possible even within what appears on the surface to be a compactly organised group. It is also worth pointing out that many of those who would suffer torture rather than admit themselves to be 'religious' (and who object violently to being told that they are, let us say, 'anonymous Christians'), have in very many cases rejected, not the values connected with religion, but the organised forms which it has taken. As rationalists and humanists never tire of pointing out, the outward paraphernalia of religion are in no way necessary for the living of a human life on sound ethical principles. Nor are they necessary in respect of 'transcendental' experiences – for instance, those connected with music, art, nature, human relations, and the like.

To observations of this kind the believer reacts in a variety of ways, depending in the last resort on where he or she believes the ultimate source of authority in religion to lie. If authority rests in the (apparently) plain statements of a holy book, then the mere fact that the uncommited reject all or some of those statements is enough to disqualify them from ever grasping anything of value. But at the opposite extreme, to place the seat of authority in the individual's exercise of the principle of free inquiry does not lead to any such consequences. Rather the opposite, since such a stance is capable of opening up the widest perspectives, virtually irrespective of formal commitment to one tradition rather than another.

However, the question here is whether non-commitment is a

positive advantage in regard to the study of religion. Here again I think that one must ask 'non-commitment to *what*, precisely?'

If one takes up a stance which involves the assumption that there is no supernatural (or transcendent) order of being, that there has never been such an order of being, and that those who have affirmed their belief in it (in whatever forms) have done so purely on account of past human immaturity and error, then the outlook is not bright. It is not that the student who takes such a position has no right to study religion: if this were the case, then many departments of religious studies (and a few of theology) would be decimated at a stroke. It is rather the case that in the absence of a supernatural or transcendent order to relate to, everything in religion must perforce be referred to some other cause, and the student will never be able to take anything which the believer says at its face value. Nothing is explained: everything has to be explained away. Religion individually is a product of undernourishment, the ingestion of poisons and the fear of death. Institutionally it is a constellation of power and property, prepared to fight when its bailiwick is threatened and reducing the people to order by 'supernatural sanctions' when normal means of persuasion fail.

It is precisely this which Marxist historians of religion claim, and which they lose no opportunity of asserting. To be sure, one may still study religion, but only as one would study the social conditions of feudal society – not as an example to be imitated, but as a description of what has been left behind and a warning of what 'the enemy' wishes to perpetuate. Of course, not all radically uncommitted students are Marxists. But they find themselves nevertheless in a similar situation, of being unable to allow the religious voice to speak for itself without constantly superimposing upon it values of their own. In this regard they are little different from the fundamentalist Christian or Muslim, whose commitment is too specifically bound to a single source of religious authority to permit the genuine appreciation of anything which does not fit it *expressis verbis*.

But not all commitment is of this kind, and we must take a moment to look at an interesting borderline case, which I shall call 'Commitment to relativity'.

Commitment to relativity

It is by no means unusual in these days to find students (and others) occupying a position which is at one and the same time positive toward religion-in-general and negative toward religion-in-particular, expecially when the latter has anything to do with traditional Christianity. (The traditional religions of the geographical East, on the other hand, fare much better.) On this view, if there is transcendental 'truth' in religion, then it is best not to try to pin it down too tightly. Above all what must not be done is to imagine that it can be limited to the deliverances of any one religious tradition. Very likely the truth-content of all individual religions is much the same everywhere in so far as they contribute to the better understanding of the world and man's place in it. All offer experiences of self-transcendence, ethical injunctions, social organisation and intellectual reflection: the first two are 'of the essence', while the third and fourth are culturally conditioned, and therefore more or less unimportant.

Where there have been quarrels among believers, these have almost invariably been caused by the failure to distinguish between essence and cultural options: the latter have been supposed to be the former, with fatal consequences all round. Essentially, therefore, the only absolute truth is that the religious traditions to which people commit themselves are relative – relative to one another and relative to Absolute Truth (which is in any case probably attainable only by vision). Most would allow that in this general sense, Absolute Truth is one – though the sense is so general that 'the one' may appear to have no precise content at all. But the kaleidoscopic visions of the religions separately owe more to the windows through which 'the one' is viewed than to the nature of the Ultimate Reality.

To claim anything more than this for the tradition to which the believer is committed is a common but regrettable error. To study religion is then to unmask the error – to distinguish between essence and manifestations in such a way as to retain the absoluteness of the former by drawing attention to the false claims made on behalf of the latter.

A view very like this is held by a great many Hindus. Following the example of Sri Ramakrishna at the end of the nineteenth century, they claim that all religions are equally capable of leading the devotee to the threshold of Ultimate Reality, but that once this threshold is crossed, all such distinctions vanish in the undifferentiated One. The traditions do not and cannot 'contain' Truth: they can but point in its general direction. And the gross error committed by many religionists is not that they seek a pathway to the truth – for if they did not do that, they would scarcely be religionists at all – but that they identify their own particular pathway with the goal to which it points. Most Hindus are convinced that Christianity and Islam have been equally at fault in this regard. But they in fact go beyond this position in many cases, to claim that since Hinduism has been the only great religion to recognise the relativity of all religions, it is therefore intellectually and spiritually superior to all its competitors.

How common this general attitude is in the West today every educationalist knows. Again and again less than fully committed students of religion are found turning away from any form of 'exclusive' religion and accepting the relativist point of view. That it makes the teaching of comparative religion easy we all know – even in secondary schools. That it makes the teaching of the Judaeo-Christian traditions difficult many of us also know: in that area 'the committed' will absorb whatever one cares to teach them, while everyone else will erect a virtually impregnable barrier. Their commonest word for non-relativity is 'arrogance'.

But it is not arrogance. It is merely the normal and natural consequence of the acceptance of a total life-stance – a totally explicit set of values which affect everything, in this world and (in its own terms) beyond it. Often what I have called 'commitment to relativity' is not actually total commitment at all. It is an intellectual position which, though it certainly has some ethical consequences, makes no personal demands on the individual, and of itself mediates little of the transcendent. The case of the 'mystics' (assuming that they can be identified) is different: they have passed *through* a tradition to the ineffable One, and in most cases, even after having reached the One, return again and again to the 'mundane observables' of their tradition for spiritual sustenance. St. John of the Cross did not abandon the Mass; even Shankaracharya wrote hymns in 'mythological' terms to Siva; Sadhu Sundar Singh did not throw away his Bible in between his ecstasies and visions. The modern semi-secular religious relativism seldom passes through traditions; rather its circumvents, if it does not ignore them. And it is able to do this not least because it flourishes in a secular context, among those whose view of institutional and dogmatic religion oscillates between alienation from the close-at-hand and nostalgia for the remote and culturally unattainable.

Commitment to relativity, in short, is not altogether what it seems, in that it does not affirm the equality of religious traditions as they are, but only the equality of what a certain type of mind has been able to distil out of them. As a rule, a determined effort to grasp the essentials of any individual tradition (and every tradition, great or small, is unique, each in its own way) makes a totally comprehensive relativism difficult, if not impossible to hold.

Total commitment

To speak of religious commitment is, as we have said, a more modern phenomenon in the world of religion than most people realise. To think in this way always involves the assumption that the individual has a free choice in the matter, that evidence has been weighed and that a decision has been arrived at freely and without compulsion. In western Christian terms, one 'attends the church of one's choice' (though the 'church' may be a synagogue, a mosque, a temple or a meditation centre). One accepts some religious teachings, and rejects others, one joins one group rather than another, adopts one scale of values rather than another. It is therefore up to each group of believers to exhibit its credentials, and up to each mature individual to decide whether to accept them.

It is further assumed that entry into such a group is by way of 'conversion' – an individual experience in which absolute conviction is attained (either intellectually or emotionally, or with the two in combination), the discredited past is rejected and a new life begun. Of course there are other standards of membership, and the children of believers are brought up to accept the values of the community to which their parents belong. But, again in modern Western terms, this is widely regarded as something less than full commitment. Faith inherited is, if not bogus faith, a tame acquiescence in the convictions of others until such time as a conscious personal decision for or against has been arrived at.

But for this pattern to be acceptable at all, it is necessary to reckon with the very real possibility that the individual is free to opt out of religious life altogether; and with the further assumption that religion is a purely personal matter which bears little or no relation to the ways in which the community orders its affairs in other areas of life. It is in other words a by-product of the secularisation process (which we shall discuss separately in Chapter eight). If the individual is totally free to be committed or not, then that commitment presumably does not produce anti-social behaviour. Where commitment of a certain kind is popularly believed to lead to anti-social behaviour (as in the case of a few of today's 'new religious movements') then society may take steps to try to prevent it taking place.

Need it be pointed out that in other parts of the world than the industrial West, religious allegiance is either not a question of free choice at all, or is permitted as a matter of free choice only to the extent to which it restricts its activities to the private sector? With some few exceptions, to be, say, a Hindu or a Muslim (or even a Roman Catholic) today is not to have chosen in a free market, but to have been born in a particular part of the world and under a specific law. Or that in the People's Republic of China or the German Democratic Republic, religion is permitted only to the extent to which it does not interfere with affairs of state? The canopy of Jewishness stretches over far more than the contents of the Talmud, covering as it does the entire collective memory of a people's history and culture.

Now the point of all this is that the Western, largely evangelically Christian-inspired fashion of speaking of religion in terms of deliberate 'commitment' may make sense only within a religious free-trade area. But allowing that it does make sense there, and that the argument is for better or worse 'Western' at this point, what are its implications as far as the *study* of religion is concerned?

The argument that the totally committed believer is unable to understand his own tradition, because he is too close to it, and unable to understand anyone else's, because he is not close enough, is not uncommon. But is not the whole force of this objection dissipated, if 'understand' should turn out to mean something different in the two cases? If I may be permitted a biblical illustration, there is an episode in the Gospel of John (ch. 9), in which a blind man is healed by Jesus. Jesus' opponents try to make the man acknowledge that Jesus is 'a sinner', and that he has been healed by God direct. The man answers: 'Whether he is a sinner, I do not know; one thing I know, that though I was blind, now I see'

(9:25). Of *intellectual* understanding there is nothing in this episode; there is on the other hand a deep personal consciousness of a change in life's conditions, which I am disposed to take as a prototype of the 'conversion experience'. Something has happened; a radical change has been brought about, in face of which intellectual considerations are strictly irrelevant. To this I may add one further illustration, of a conversation with a young follower of a popular Hindu *guru* (which one is of no importance). I asked him whether he accepted the *guru* because of the 'truths' he taught, or accepted certain teachings as true because the *guru* taught them; without hesitation he replied that everything the *guru* taught was 'true', and that the content of his message was not open to discussion. Having placed complete trust in his person, everything else followed.

But in what sense is this 'understanding'? Hardly at all, if by 'understanding' we mean a process in which a certain distance is placed between the student and the phenomenon studied, and in which the student attempts to bring certain rules of cause and effect to bear on the questions under investigation. In this context, 'commitment' means total trust – in a person, in a community, in a tradition, in a scripture, or in a combination of all four. Total trust of this order is not a matter for discussion: one either trusts, or one does not. One would hope that even those who know what it is to experience trust of this order would be able to conceive that others might perchance be committed to some other authority in life's final questions. Where they are, they make good students of religion. Where they are not (and very often they are not), their studies proceed safely only along the paths which their tradition lays down for them, and to leave those paths means total disorientation.

To this we may perhaps add one further general comment. Because commitment of the kind I have tried briefly to describe often results from a process in which the emotions play a considerable part, every attempt to raise 'cause and effect' (that is, rational) questions is liable to cause an instinctive emotional reaction on the believer's part. If commitment is a total life-stance, then to bring up the question of alternative life-stances is almost always seen as an attack on one's personal integrity. That it may also involve the calling in question of one's cherished authorities simply makes things worse. In this, religion is not a special case. The phenomenon is well known in politics and among environmental groups; while the combination of all three which we sometimes encounter in today's world heaps commitment on commitment, potential aggression on potential aggression, in a frightening manner. I still recall the scandalised reception given to a cheerfully irreverent nutritionist by an intense group of modern dieticians, as they heard him blaspheme all their gods, one after another. We all know what happens to those who attempt to communicate an unpopular political message to assemblies of the faithful: they are simply shouted down, almost irrespective of what they actually say. Companies of religious believers are seldom exposed directly to this kind of frontal assault; but that most are well used to long-range artillery tactics where their identity is threatened, is common knowledge.

Does this then mean that commitment and understanding are two entirely different functions of the human mind, the one emotional and the other rational, the one existential and the other intellectual? Although in many cases it certainly seems so, and although there are many individuals in whom the one positively excludes the other, there is no absolute reason why it should be so. The human mind is not so easily compartmentalised into areas marked 'emotion' and 'reason', 'art' and 'science', 'subconscious' and 'conscious'. Commitment may be understood, without ceasing to be commitment. Equally, one may be deeply (even passionately) committed to a quest for understanding, in religion as in all else.

In the end, though, one must allow that whereas commitment may come in a flash (though this is not to say that it may not be years in the making), understanding is a slow process, and one which may never be complete. It calls for discipline, care, the painstaking gathering of evidence, the ability to compare, and a desire for accuracy. But this is not all, for it also requires a further quality, or combination of qualities, which one is almost tempted to say cannot be learned, though they can no doubt be cultivated.

Precisely what they are to be called is a moot point. These days in the study of religion we speak fairly often of 'sympathy' and 'empathy', and mean the attempt to enter in some way into the emotions of others, rejoicing with those who rejoice and weeping with those who weep, dancing with those who dance and meditating with those who meditate. More technically, we sometimes use the two 'phenomenological' terms *epoché* (the suspension of judgment) and *eidetic vision* (the capacity to see things as wholes). In the end, we trust that by these means we shall be able to see something of what is essential in religion, not in spite of the oddities of individual believers, but through the eyes of those who believe – or if you prefer, those who are committed.

But this is not a quest for intellectual understanding carried out from a great height, as though the student were totally immune to the religious imperative. On the contrary: because it recognises that in matters of religion, human variety is human first and varied only incidentally, it believes that the student can by this means find his or her place in the human religious panorama, while acknowledging 'the others' less as competitors than as fellow human beings. But because in this sense, no *total* religious tradition enjoys 'most favoured religion' status, it is still met with less than full approval from the side of those whose religious commitment is sharply focused.

However, the 'phenomenologist' of religion is not greatly disturbed thereby. He does not see this enterprise as the enemy of commitment as such (though it must be acknowledged that there are types of commitment which can be approached only with some difficulty). In studying the anatomy, physiology and psychology of religion, the student is trying to look at some human fundamentals, and to find out how the human mechanism works. It is not primarily his business to join one of two banner-waving crowds (or for that matter a police force paid to keep the two apart).

I am not going to be so rash as to try to identify this exercise as an art or as a science; it contains elements of both. But it certainly involves the mastery of a craft. Those who have been committed know what it is like to wave banners, even though they may have abandoned the practice. Those who have never been religiously committed (though they may have a powerful commitment to no-religion) lose on the roundabouts what they gain on the swings, and find it hard to disguise their sense of superiority. Those who are deeply committed have been known to be unable to appreciate anyone's commitment save their own. It is the misfortune of the student that he or she is faced with more hard work than any, since there are so many human beings, and they all have the right to be listened to. To listen is an art; to grasp what they are saying involves both a craft and a science. But unless the student feels the force of arguments on more than one side, it is likely that a point somewhere has been missed.

Three

The Question of Definition

There are two broad alternatives in the study of religion. One ('theology') centres on the material preserved and treasured within a single historical tradition. The other ('religious studies') is prepared, at least in principle, to widen its field of vision so as to gain a total view of human beings the world over, involved in certain forms of belief and behaviour. There is of course a 'definition' of a kind implicit in both these activities, since in either case it is simply assumed that what is being studied is 'religion'. To spend time discussing definitions of religion might therefore appear to be time wasted, were it not for the fact that one soon discovers in reading or discussion that there is very real disagreement, among believers and students alike, about where religion actually begins and ends. Time and time again, a writer on religion will begin by saying, in effect, 'Before I get on with my subject, let me tell you what I understand by religion.' A day's work in an average library would produce several dozen statements resulting from this need for explicitness. But what kind of statements are they?

Some serve a strictly descriptive purpose, and these we may call 'working definitions', intended to facilitate identification and study. But others – and these are more common – serve a different purpose. C.S. Lewis warns us that: '... when we leave the dictionaries we must view all definitions with grave distrust ... Unless we are writing a dictionary, or a text-book of some technical subject, we define our words only because we are in some measure departing from their real current sense. Otherwise there would be no purpose in doing so' (Lewis, 1960: 18). Many such forms of words, again according to Lewis, are really 'tactical definitions', produced in the heat of controversy. A tactical definition tells us little or nothing about the actual meaning of a term, though it may tell us a great deal about the person producing it.

There are many tactical definitions of religion, some of them very well known – for instance Karl Marx's statement about religion being 'the opium of the people', or the French rationalist Salomon Reinach's scornful epitome of religion as 'a sum of scruples which prevent the free exercise of our faculties'. Neither is without point; yet neither *describes* anything. For tactical definitions serve mainly a polemical purpose, to the delight of the supporters of the Cause and the annoyance of its enemies. They may be clever, barbed, witty; but they do not describe. They merely epitomise.

Descriptive, or working definitions, on the other hand, seldom emerge easily or spontaneously, and where religion is concerned, their subject-matter is so complex that they can seldom be terse, pithy or succinct.

Sixty years ago, A.S. Geden wrote in a popular handbook that 'It is admittedly difficult to present a satisfactory definition of "religion"; nor is the problem rendered any more easy by the fact that most men think they know what it is' (Geden, 1922: 16). And as though this were not enough, scholars also have a habit of assuming that whatever their readers may think they know about the subject, actually they do *not* know what they are about to be told. They assume religion to be this or that; but actually it is something else. William James, for instance, in his classic study *The Varieties of Religious Experience*, seemed to assume that most of his readers would begin by assuming that religion was mainly a matter of 'going to church'. This being so, he produced an 'arbitrary' definition of religion as '... the feelings, acts, and experiences of individual men in their solitude, so far as they apprehend themselves to stand in relation to whatever they may consider the divine' (James, 1902: 31). Of course James knew well enough that 'religion' as a term was capable of embracing more than that. But since his purpose in that particular book was to discuss *individual* religious experience, he produced a 'definition' to serve as a statement of intent. It was not intended to serve as a comprehensive working definition.

A similar form of words was used, twenty or so years later, by Alfred North Whitehead, in his book *Religion in the Making:* 'Religion is what the individual does with his own solitariness,' he wrote. If a man has never been solitary, Whitehead argued, he has never been religious (Whitehead, 1926: 16). These words have often been treated as though they were a working definition of religion, though in fact they are nothing of the kind: once more they are an aphorism, an epigram *about* religion, intended not to describe a visible phenomenon but to isolate a particular aspect and set it up as normative. Very probably Whitehead had James' words in mind; but he made them fulfil a different purpose. Whereas James was telling his readers what aspect or aspects of religion he was preparing to deal with in a book devoted explicitly to the study of religious experience, Whitehead was attempting to characterize something about the essence of religion as he saw it. His book contains many such epigrams, though it is this which has most often been isolated and quoted out of context, and which has therefore stuck in the minds of generations of readers as Whitehead's 'definition of religion'.

Evidently, therefore, 'definitions of religion' may serve different purposes, depending on the particular intentions and presuppositions of whoever formulates them. Doubtless tactical definitions and working definitions alike will all tell us *something* about religion in one or other of its aspects; but generally speaking the former will tell us rather more about the state of mind of their creator than about observable phenomena. In this regard the word 'religion' functions in ways very similar to words like 'art' and 'music'. The way in which they are understood varies so much in different areas, cultures and periods that idiosyncratic variations are only to be expected. There is also the 'Humpty Dumpty principle', as stated by Lewis Carroll in *Alice through the Looking-Glass*:

> 'There's glory for you!' [said Humpty Dumpty].
>
> 'I don't know what you mean by "glory",' Alice said.
>
> Humpty Dumpty smiled contemptuously. 'Of course you don't – till I tell you. I meant, "There's a nice knock-down argument for you!"'
>
> 'But "glory" doesn't mean "A nice knock-down argument",' Alice objected.
>
> 'When *I* use a word,' Humpty Dumpty said, in rather a scornful tone, 'it means just what I choose it to mean – neither more nor less.'
>
> 'The question is,' said Alice, 'whether you *can* make words mean so many different things.'
>
> 'The question is,' said Humpty Dumpty, 'which is to be master – that's all.'
>
> Alice was much too puzzled to say anything ...

Words of a certain kind may on this principle mean anything that one chooses that they should mean; they may on the other hand mean nothing in particular, or be endlessly reiterated without anyone knowing, or remembering precisely what they may originally have meant (like 'democratic' or 'polyunsaturated').

Some years ago I happened upon 'A Vocabulary of Terms in use at Clark University' – in use, that is, earlier this century in the wake of Transcendentalism and in the early heyday of the psychology of religion. 'Religion' the *Vocabulary* described as 'a sentiment of reverence and acquiescence in some consensus concerning fundamental questions'. It added: 'N.B. Religion includes nothing within the limits of any creed or cult.' Although it was clearly not intended that this form of words should be taken too seriously, it deserves a mention here, if for no other reason that it appears actually to describe the way in which 'religion' was discussed in that place and at that time. It is of course not a definition at all. At most it is a tongue-in-check characterisation of a temporary intellectual fashion. But is it not worth bearing in mind as a warning that the partisan observer may appear to be discussing 'religion', while yet at the same time adjusting the content of the term to that which he is capable of comprehending and accepting – in this case a vague consensus concerning ill-defined fundamentals? The practice is not an uncommon one, even today.

Of course one might feel that this point is simply not worth discussing. But the tendency is there, to make 'religion' mean neither more nor less than what a person chooses that it should mean, irrespective of the whole host of observables which can be identified on other criteria as belonging within the orbit of religious belief and behaviour. Far safer is the advice given again by Alfred North Whitehead (a useful corrective, incidentally, to the isolation from its context of his remark about religion being purely the individual's reactions to the experience of solitude):

> We are dealing with a topic, complex and many-sided. It comprises the deliverances of the understanding as it harmonises our deepest intuitions. It comprises emotional responses to formulations of thought and to modes of behaviour. It cuts into every aspect of human existence. So far as concerns religious problems, simple solutions are bogus solutions ... We must not postulate simplicity. (Whitehead, 1933: 165).

If we take this warning to heart, and try to avoid postulating simplicity (such as beginning our statements with the words 'religion is nothing but ...'), is there any form of words which we can use in order to *describe* – not to epitomise or condense – exactly what it is we are setting out to study?

If a definition involves, as the *Concise Oxford Dictionary* tells us, making a statement about 'the precise nature of a thing or meaning of a word', then we are at once brought up against some serious difficulties. The 'thing' or 'phenomenon' – that which can be observed or identified – differs so enormously from time to time and from place to place that common denominators may be exceedingly difficult to find. Between a Quaker meeting in New England and a fertility ritual in New Caledonia there is more than geographical distance. These differences may of course be 'explained', at least in part, in 'cultural' terms – but this simply forces us sideways, into another equally difficult and disputed area, that of 'culture'.

The phrase 'the meaning of a word' is also problematical. Words are not static. They shift in meaning, shade into one another, execute U-turns, wander from language to language, picking up and shedding meaning *en route*. Simple substantives like man, woman, door, table, tree, mountain, can change their meaning only within narrow limits. But as soon as a word comes to have reference, however slight or indirect, to subjective states of mind the difficulties are multiplied. 'Beauty', 'wisdom' and 'justice' may serve as cases in point – none of which can be defined without reference to what the individual actually *believes* these things to be.

The dual aspect of religion – that it involves both outward practices and inward convictions – has been recognised for long enough. Earlier this century S.A. Cook observed that '[w]e may regard religion as a body of beliefs and practices which control or shape or influence a certain portion of human thought and activity ...' But he was also forced to add: 'Or we may regard religion as bound up with the profounder side of the consciousness ...' (Cook, 1914: 33). Definitions will often by their very inadequacy reflect an over-emphasis on one or the other side of this alliance. William James, as we have seen, chose to eliminate the institutional from his working definition. Emile Durkheim did precisely the opposite when he wrote that '... religion should be an eminently collective thing' and made this statement:

> When a certain number of sacred things sustain relations of co-ordination or subordination with each other in such a way as to form a system, having a certain unity, but which is not comprised within any other system of the same sort, the totality of these beliefs and their corresponding rites constitutes a religion. (Durkheim, 1915: 41).

Characteristically, he was describing 'a religion' (which he elsewhere called 'a unified system of beliefs and practices relative to sacred things'), and not attempting to define 'religion-as-such'. His concern was with religious organisations, and less with whatever beliefs, experiences or convictions they might sustain.

Relatively few modern definitions of religion are of this type, however. Most attempt to approach the question from the angle of belief, either subjectively, through the mental processes involved in 'belief' or 'faith', or objectively, in terms of the nature and attributes of what is believed in. The anthropologist E.B. Tylor's celebrated 'minimum definition of religion' as 'the belief in Spiritual Beings' (Tylor, 1929, I: 424) may serve as a case in point. A further subjective element was added by Allan Menzies, when he defined religion as 'the worship of higher powers from a sense of need' (Menzies, 1922: 13). The principle was carried further by George Galloway in the 1930s; religion, he stated, is 'Man's faith in a power beyond himself whereby he seeks to satisfy emotional needs and gain stability of life, and which he expresses in acts of worship and service' (Galloway, 1935: 184).

The implication here is that there is in religion a central core, or essence, of belief, and that from that centre, there have spread concentric circles of behaviour and institutional organisation. But at the centre there is *belief* or *faith*, which is produced in response to men's emotional and psychical need. However, this again is less a description than an analysis, and it leaves virtually untouched whatever collective aspects may have in the course of time gathered around this central core.

It is perhaps not surprising that where psychologists have attempted to define religion, they have done so very largely in terms of the workings of the individual mind. In his book *A Psychological Study of Religion* (1912), the Swiss-American psychologist J.H. Leuba assembled a large number of existing forms of words which could be classified as definitions; mainly, one suspects, in order to demonstrate the fallibility of their originators in the realm of psychology. Elsewhere he was to state that '... the amazing discrepancies and contradictions offered by authorised [though who authorised them he does not say] definitions of Religion arise, in my opinion, primarily from a faulty psychology' (Leuba, 1915: 5). Accordingly he breaks down the working of the human mind into the three areas of willing, feeling and thinking, and analyses religion on this basis.

This was plausible enough (or it seemed so, in the days of pre-Freudian psychology), but again it took no real account of the collective, behavioural modes in which religion expresses itself. Perhaps individual piety might be dealt with this way; but what was omitted, was any attempt to cope with that in religion which passes beyond individual personality into the lives of families, tribes, castes and nations.

It is all too easily forgotten by western students that many languages simply do not have an equivalent of the word 'religion' in their vocabulary. 'Law', 'duty', 'custom', 'worship', 'spiritual discipline', 'the way' they know: 'religion' they do not. In recent years, where non-western traditions have thought in 'religious' terms, they have often done so through the medium of some European language. A Hindu writing in English may be happy enough to speak of 'religion': in Sanskrit, Hindi, or Tamil he must use words having a different connotation.

The trouble here is that the Latin word *religio*, from which our 'religion' is of course derived, is not only a neutral, descriptive term. It has strong overtones of a political and moral nature. When the Roman writers used it, they were not describing something, but rather setting bounds to something. Occasional attempts were made, by Cicero and Lactantius among others, to argue about its meaning on the basis of where it had come from. Cicero derived *religio* from the verb *relegere*, 'to re-read', Lactantius from *religare*, 'to bind fast', and there is no way of knowing which was right. In the latter case, *religio* would then have meant 'that which binds men and women to one another and to the gods'; in the former, it would also have involved that which is re-read, that is, passed on along chains of tradition.

Either seems acceptable enough, until we remember the firm distinction drawn by Cicero (and others) between *religio* and *superstitio* – a distinction which in a slightly confused form is still with us. According to Cicero, *religio* contained *deorum cultu pio* (the pious worship of the gods). It involved *pietas* (piety), *sanctitas* (holiness) and the sound and sober reverence of those dieties accepted by the state. *Superstitio* on the other hand, involved *timor inanis deorum* (the unreasoning fear of the gods), and as such was unhelpful to the individual and more seriously, positively harmful to the body politic. We may perhaps recall than in ancient Greece, to question the worship offered to the Olympian deities was to be an 'atheist', as Socates discovered to his cost. Again, the dividing line passed between what was *officially* acceptable within the bounds of a particular social and political organisation, and what was not. The early Christians in the Roman Empire were similarly called 'atheists', not because they believed in no God, but because from the Roman point of view they believed in the wrong God.

It may be to pass from the classically sublime to the faintly ridiculous, but when, in his novel *Tom Jones*, Henry Fielding makes Parson Thwackum say, 'When I mention religion, I mean the Christian religion; and not only the Christian religion, but the Protestant religion; and not only the Protestant religion, but the Church of England', he is stating substantially the same principle. Religion, on this view, exists primarily in order to give coherence to a social organism or culture, and to pass beyond that culture, either spiritually or intellectually, is to pass into chaos or atheism. To worship is to revere, not necessarily the maker of the world, but the acknowledged maker of the tribe, city, state or community. The supernaturals who were acknowledged on the individual level of 'superstition' were not unimportant on the local level: but they had 'made' nothing, least of all the state. Superstition is therefore political, as well as religious, nonconformity, in which the solemn assembly is replaced by unnecessary and unreasoning fear, Cicero's *timor superfluus et delirius*.

However, nothing can be identified as a disease unless there is first some idea of what constitutes health. The Roman labelled as 'superstition' all that did not conform to the formal, legalistic and conservative state orthodoxy and orthopraxy. Seventeen or eighteen centuries later, the Christian did the same over against the myths, rituals, tabus, sacrifices and prayers of the greater part of the world, drawing the very same kind of distinction as the Greeks had done between 'Hellenes' and 'Barbarians', as that between 'Jews' and 'Gentiles', and as that drawn by the Chinese between the 'Middle

Kingdom' and the rest of the world. And even tribes, let us remember, often called themselves 'the people' – the Bantu, the Inuit (Eskimos), 'das Volk' – the implication being that whatever is outside the charmed circle exists only at a lower level of awareness, in a dimension in which life is ungoverned, and perhaps ungovernable. Inside the circle there is order, and there is the gift of life, given by the supernaturals and shaped by law: outside there are only (literally) 'the lesser breeds without the law'. They may regulate their lives as they please. They cannot regulate them perfectly. Unreasoning superstition is regulated only by fear; religion (or more properly, *religio*) is regulated by reverence for a divinely-established, and therefore 'true', order of things.

The word *religio*, therefore, does not tell us what religion is; it tells us initially only what the classical Roman culture considered that it ought to be. As well as the due reverence which it was the duty of every Roman citizen to pay to the official deities of the state, the word *religio* could be used to refer to an oath or to any other sacred duty, to personal piety or to any of the rituals and customs that have to do with the worship of the gods. And during the long period of Latin Christianity, the word continued to be used in broadly the same sense. It is true that Christian authors were able to speak of *religiones* in the plural, meaning by this other patterns of ritual and belief; and that Luther was able to speak of 'the old religion' as standing in contrast to the faith which he proclaimed. But still there remained a close bond between *religio* and what a particular social organism found acceptable; in modern terms, *religio* expressed not 'religion' as a universal form of human behaviour related to the sacred, but '*a* religion' – a circumscribed form of belief and social organisation related to the ethics and structure of a particular culture or group of cultures.

*

In Christianity, and still more in the great Eastern traditions, the emphasis is somewhat different. Again we do not have cause to review all the evidence, but some points may be made. 'Religion' is a word which occurs seldom in either the Old or the New Testaments; but where it does occur in English translations, it always renders words which mean not a systematic collection of statements *about*

God, but a living relationship *to* God within the terms of a 'covenant' or 'testament'.

The commonest Greek word which the English Bible usually translates as 'religion' is *threskeia* – a submission before, and worship of, God, together with the consequences of that submission. In Acts 26:5, for instance, the Apostle Paul is represented as saying that 'according to the strictest party of our religion I have lived as a Pharisee'. Here the emphasis is clearly on ritual and moral observance. The ethical element is stated still more clearly in James 1:27, where we read that 'Religion that is pure and undefiled before God and the Father is this: to visit orphans and widows in their affliction, and to keep oneself unstained from the world.'

But the New Testament also has a word for 'superstition', *deisidaimonia* (the fear of lesser supernaturals). However, things are complicated somewhat by its irregular use. Again to take two examples from the Acts of the Apostles, on the one hand we find a Roman using it of Judaism ('... they had certain points of dispute with him about their own superstition and about one Jesus ...', Acts 25:19), and on the other, Paul is made to use it of a miscellaneous collection of Greek dilettantes. In Acts 17:22, he tells the men of Athens, 'I perceive that in all things you are too superstitious' (this in the Authorised Version: the Revised Standard Version confuses things by translating the operative word 'very religious').

We do not need to prolong this inquiry further. The important thing to remember is that, to the ancient world, 'religion' was a matter involving not the individual's inward experiences of 'the holy', but the attitudes, rituals and moral conventions on which a particular society and culture rested. Certainly God (and the gods and goddesses) were there; certainly they exercised power along the channels of the sacred. But they could only be spoken of in one's own language, so to speak, and they could only be approached on the conditions which they had themselves laid down, through a network of sacred laws and obligations. To accept those obligations and to submit to those laws was to acknowledge one's place in the divinely-ordained scheme of things. Outsiders, on the other hand, were not expected to do so. This was not to say that they had no divine sanctions of their own; simply that these would inevitably be different sanctions: 'For all the peoples walk each in the name of its god, but we will walk in the name of the Lord our God for ever and ever' (Micah 4:5).

*

As we have already noted most non-Western languages initially lack words which correspond in intention and application to 'religion'; therefore, words belonging to the same general area can be 'defined' only in terms of the disciplines they presuppose, since most refer to paths to be followed or to rules to be obeyed.

To the Hindu, for instance, the operative Sanskrit word is *dharma*, which may be variously (and inadequately) rendered into English as 'truth', 'duty', 'law', 'order' and 'right'. The implications of *dharma* involve the whole of Hindu belief and practice, stretching all the way from private propriety to public law, from temple and household ritual to caste obligation. Basically it refers, however, to a cosmic order, to which the individual may or may not conform, but which possesses its own intrinsic norms and conventions, to which the individual is expected to conform as part of a wider social order. In practice, however, the term *dharma* is qualified in various ways. It may be 'Indianized' as *Hindu dharma* or *Arya* (noble) *dharma*, or 'universalised' as *sanatana dharma* (the eternal rule). It may be supplemented by the use of such words as *sadhana* (discipline) or *marga* (pathway). It may reach a high degree of social explicitness in the compound term *varnaśramadharma* – which denotes the *dharma* observed in the rule of caste (*varna*) and in the four stages of life (*aśrama*) through which the Brahmin is expected to pass. It may even be qualified in the expression *mleccha dharma* to mean 'foreign *dharma*', i.e. non-Hindu belief and practice. The basic point of reference, however, is always to a religious, and very largely ethnic norm, resting on the foundations of Vedic revelation, to which foreigners are not expected to subscribe (though in modern Hindu belief, all *dharmas* are theoretically regarded as being of equal value as pathways to the threshold of the Real, *Hindu dharma* being binding only on those born within a particular context).

The Buddhist Pali term *dhamma* is similar in its scope and implications, though with a weaker ethnic reference. The Buddha, it is maintained, did not invent the *dhamma* (which in Buddhist terms comes to approximate more closely to the notion of 'discipline'); he merely rediscovered it after long ages of neglect. It has a stronger doctrinal focus than does the Hindu *dharma*, resting as it does on the teachings of Gautama the Buddha, summed up in the Four

Excellent Truths and the Excellent Eight-fold Path. But it also involves an ideal life, either as a monk or a nun, or as a layman who accepts a modified form of the discipline. The full Buddhist term for what the West calls 'Buddhism' is in fact 'The Doctrine and the Discipline' – the Doctrine (*dhamma*) expounding man's nature and the conditions of human life, and the Discipline laying down the conditions on which man may escape from its limitations and its suffering. The confession 'I take refuge in the Buddha; I take refuge in the Doctrine; I take refuge in the Community' sums up a typical pattern, of a Teacher or Mediator, the content of what is taught, and the community within which the teachings are passed on. It is sometimes argued that because Buddhism does not admit the existence of a Supreme Being, it therefore cannot be a religion – the assumption being that a 'religion' must be defined in terms of theistic belief. But Buddhism is equally a way of approaching the transcendent; it is equally a value-system, a statement of what values are, and what are not, ultimate; it is equally a focus of spiritual discipline and a striving toward self-transcendence; and in some cases it is clearly a *religio* – a scale of social values based on transcendent values.

*

In the recent study of religion, as in the 'comparative religion' of the past, numerous delimiting definitions of religion have been produced, not least by anthropologists. Often they concentrate on the culturally determined aspects of religion. Melford E. Spiro defines religion as 'an institution of culturally patterned interaction with culturally postulated superhuman beings' (1965: 96). J. Milton Yinger is less precise, writing that religion may be defined as 'a system of beliefs and practices by means of which a group of people struggle with ... ultimate problems of human life' (1970: 7). Most explicit is Clifford Geertz, according to whom religion is

(1) A system of symbols which acts to
(2) establish powerful, pervasive and longlasting moods and motivations in men by
(3) formulating conceptions of a general order of existence and
(4) clothing these conceptions with such an aura of factuality that
(5) the moods and motivations seem uniquely realistic (1965: 42).

Although all of these are functionally useful, and turn our attention to symbol-systems and cultural patterns, in every case one is left with the suspicion that, in point of fact, there is no transcendent order there to be related to. Superhuman beings are only 'culturally postulated'; conceptions about human existence have only 'an aura of factuality'. It is perhaps not out of place to suggest that whatever the Western rationalist may think or believe, to the religious believer, the supernatural being in which he resposes his trust (or which he fears) actually exists, and that it is up to the student of religion, not to pour scorn on his belief or demonstrate that the unsophisticated believer simply has to be mistaken, but to understand the modes and the practical consequences of that belief. It was W. Brede Kristensen who reminded us many years ago that there exists no other religious reality than the faith of the believer; and it is at that point that the student must approach religion. To impose value-judgments upon belief will inevitably mean that it is dealt with in terms other than those which it establishes for itself. That we must try to avoid.

For this reason, in the last analysis only value-free descriptive definitions are of use to the student. As an example we may quote a form of words assembled by the American psychologist of religion J.B. Pratt, who in 1920 defined religion as 'the serious and social attitude of individuals or communities toward the power or powers which they conceive as having ultimate control over their interests and destinies' (1920: 2).

*

Although so far in this chapter we have been discussing various attempts to define the term 'religion' in the singular, it is equally important to remember that the same word is used in the indefinite form '*a* religion', and in the plural, 'religions'. Again for a fuller treatment of the history of these two verbalisations in Western thought we may refer the reader to Wilfred Cantwell Smith (Smith, 1963); again we may make some general observations.

A religion is commonly held to be (in more or less the sense in which Durkheim used the word) a particular body of beliefs and practices, sufficiently well defined to be capable of carrying (in German) the suffix *-ismus* or (in English) the suffix *-ism*. Hence we have all those hordes of religious, ideological and philosophical '-isms', the existence of which has, one sometimes felt, been a dreadful barrier to clear thinking on our subject. Perhaps they are only conceptualisations; perhaps we can hardly do without them. But often they are sadly misleading. 'Buddhism' is a usable term, because of its reference to the experience and the teachings of Siddhartha Gautama, 'the Buddha' (the Enlightened One); 'Hinduism', on the other hand, refers neither to an individual teacher nor to a single accepted body of teachings, but rather to a geographical area and its inhabitants, whose religious beliefs and practices may be of the most diverse kinds. And to say 'Hinduism is a religion' may (and often does) betray a total misunderstanding of the Hindu mind, creating as it does a conceptual straitjacket within which actual Hindus are often unable to move. Many other '-isms' are equally misleading (animism, fetishism, totemism are cases in point), simply because they appear to impose rigid limits on highly flexible groups of phenomena.

A religion, in other words, whether or not it is called an '-ism', is an intellectual construction, a device through which the rationalist passion for classifying and pigeonholing expresses itself. Religion (without the article) has come to denote more or less the *genus* of which the various individual religions are considered to be *species*. In one sense, it is an abstract noun; in another, it is a collective noun. But because so many observers have been so deeply concerned to extract from the mass of available evidence some 'essential' element, the door has been thereby thrown open to the kind of pseudo-definition with which we began: 'religion' in such cases is what I consider to be most important and most essential among the welter of conflicting and contradictory human evidence which, *by common consent*, is taken to refer to the general area of human commerce with the supernatural, its ways and means, its rules and regulations, its courtesies and its horrors.

Definitions of religion, in a sense, remind one of the fable of the blind men attempting to describe an elephant. One touches its trunk and describes it as a snake; another touches its ear and describes it as a winnowing-fan; another touches its leg and describes it as a tree; another its tail and describes it as a broom.

But these men were blind. The genuine observer, whether of elephants or ordinary human beings, is not blind, nor ought he to be blinkered. And there is a great deal to be seen by the dispassionate onlooker, provided that he or she attempts to look at human phenomena as a whole, rather than at recent, convenient or subjectively attractive phenomena only. In respect of religion, modern Western man is an oddity in human history. Virtually alone of all the races of the earth, past and present, he has succeeded in dismissing from his waking mind most of the ultimate questions concerning the world he lives in and his own place in it. As a rule, he knews that these are knotty problems; but he either trusts his elders and wise men (the scientists) to explain them to him; or if they have no explanation at the moment, he assumes that answers will not be long emerging. For his priests he cares little or nothing, supposing them to have been discredited by those same scientists. Birth is mechanical and antiseptic; puberty a psychological problem; procreation a diversion; disease for the most part controllable; death a blank wall. None of these attitudes and reactions to the pattern of human life is typically human, and as soon as certain mechanical and technological supports are removed, older patterns reassert themselves. Even the absence of aspirin, or of the ready availability of food, water and shelter can return the sophisticated Westerner to the state of mind of his forgotten ancestors.

Whether that state of mind is, or is not, an adequate or accurate reaction to human life is beside the point. It is more important for our purposes to describe and account for it, for it is in this instinctive reaction to the fullness of human existence that the roots of religion are to be found.

To *define* religion is, then, far less important than to possess the ability to *recognise* it when we come across it. To impose an inadequate or one-sided tactical definition may well lead to a refusal to acknowledge whatever does not appear to conform to that definition. If religion actually is only 'what the individual does with his own solitariness', then it follows, as Whitehead recognised, that 'if you are never solitary, you are never religious' (Whitehead, 1926: 16), and that corporate aspects of religion are either of negligible importance, or of no importance at all. Valuable as it may be as an idealistic principle, this form of words is of no manner of use as a principle of recognition. In fact it has the effect of removing religion altogether from the area of observables, since all that remains of communication once you have chosen to become solitary is how you describe your experiences retrospectively; and that, as every psychologist knows, is the most unsafe testimony of all. But at the opposite extreme, if religion be defined exclusively in terms of the social forms and functions to which belief gives rise, then it will be the believer's experience which is elbowed out. Neither error is more commendable than the other.

What the student must ask is, in effect, *on what criteria* he is proposing to identify a belief, an action or an organism as 'religious'. To my mind, the only tenable criterion is that of the firm conviction *on the believer's part* (not the observer's) of the actual existence of a supernatural, supersensory order of being, and of the actual or potential interplay, through a network of sacred symbols, of that order of being with the world in which his normal life is lived. The interplay may take part on the individual or on the corporate level; it may involve rules of conduct or it may not; it may rest on an intensely personal experience or it may not; it may be intellectually worked out or it may not. But dismiss the supernatural order from the picture altogether, and you are left with sacred symbols which refer to nothing in particular. What you have left may be moral, inspiring, intellectually or aesthetically satisfying, or what you will: but it will not be religion, and some other word ought to be found to describe it.

Four
Holy Ground

Almost the first thing which the student – or indeed the casual observer – of religious affairs notices, is that 'believers' subject the times and places, the objects and personalities of the waking world to a definite scale of values. A house may be full of books; but one book is somehow different from all the others, being both handled and read in a special way. A village is full of buildings; but before entering one of them people make special preparations, while once inside, their normal behaviour changes. Men and women wearing clothes that set them apart from the crowd are treated in a manner subtly or startlingly different from workmates or the members of one's family. The days of the week are differently treated; on Fridays for some, Saturdays for others and Sundays for a third group, customary behaviour is partly or wholly suspended: travelling and trading either ceases altogether or is curtailed in favour of actions which the observer may or may not understand.

Along with these peculiarities of behaviour, the observer will note among these same groups of people characteristic attitudes – to food and drink, to war and peace, to economics, to certain animals (the cow, the pig), and to their fellow human beings generally. Members of these groups know that these attitudes to some extent set them apart from the normal man in the street, but this does not trouble them, and they may both rejoice in their standing as 'peculiar people' and take steps to persuade others to join them.

This, however, is never very easy. For one thing, because their characteristic way of life almost always makes demands which many are apt to find both old-fashioned and unreasonable. And for another, because 'believers' in fact differ greatly in what they actually believe, or claim to believe.

On the first count – and speaking now from the perspective of a Western city in the fourth quarter of the twentieth century – many people either claim not to be 'believers' at all, and therefore do not behave at all in the ways we have outlined, or they do so only sporadically. Having over a couple of centuries observed that religion has been opposed and contradicted at every turn by the practicalities of science, most have in a vague way allowed the authority of science to take the place of the authority of religion. Not that science makes no demands; but science appears not to require submission to ancient traditions, or to demand the suspension of reason. And in an age devoted to 'progress' and 'development', it may seem that religion stands for neither of these things, but for reaction and stagnation. This I believe to be a false assumption, but it is common enough for all that, and it sets intellectual limits to the spread of religious belief.

On the second count, it may seem doubtful at first sight whether there is any common ground at all between believers, since their areas of evident disagreement are so enormous. In face of these disagreements, it is common enough to find the outsider virtually throwing up his hands in despair at what appears merely to promote human disunity. Gods differ, beliefs differ, practices differ. What unites religions appears to be no more than that their adherents actually believe in *something* – a supernatural order or a map of the universe. What their respective maps represent, on the other hand, and the signs and symbols which each uses, are so wildly at variance with one another that a long and arduous course in map-reading is necessary before one can begin to grasp even one of them, let alone several.

There is more than one way in which the serious student can attempt to come to grips with the apparently infinite varieties of religious belief and practice in world history. The commonest by far is that which is perhaps a little less common than it once was, but which is still best described as 'the history of religions' ('religions' in this case stands in the plural) – an elaborate voyage of discovery through each of the world's religious traditions separately, taken in rough historical sequence. First comes whatever may be learned, or surmised, about the religious beliefs and practices of prehistoric man, usually supported by evidence drawn from peoples at a low level of material development in our world (for this to work it is necessary to accept some form of what used to be called 'the theory of survivals'). Then follow the study of those ancient civilisations which came to the attention of western scholars during the nineteenth century – Sumer and Akkad, Egypt, Persia, the Minoan-Mycenaean civilisation of Greece – and then, in an order which may vary, India, Israel, Greece and Rome, the Islamic World, China and Japan, and the development of early Christianity. Beyond this the historical student often does not go. It is perhaps unnecessary to point out that each one of these areas is in itself vast, and that this conventional list is far from complete (for instance, it seldom leaves room for the religion of the Germanic peoples, which has left a profound mark on the whole of Western culture, or for pre-Columbian America). But it has been accepted nevertheless as one way, and perhaps the best way, of approaching the study of religion on a world map. Textbook after textbook follows the same line, and discusses the same 'facts' – which are sometimes no more than intelligent guesses. This approach assumes that each religious tradition is to be understood fully only if its origins are known, that what may have happened since the European middle ages probably belongs to some other department of study, and that in the last analysis, the common ground between them is that each has been in its own way caught up in the historical process. The liberal Christian theologian may well want to add that a further, and perhaps the most important, common factor is that each tradition in its own way serves to demonstrate that God has never left himself without witness, and that each is in the light of subsequent events a *praeparatio evangelica* – which may go some way toward explaining why subsequent to the coming of Christianity on the world scene, continuing traditions (Judaism being the most obvious example) tend to be left out of the reckoning altogether, at least by conventional Christian scholarship.

However suitable this historical approach may be to the student having the time and energy to pursue each of these lines separately, and however often it has served, in a watered-down form, as a first introduction to the comparative study of religion, its self-imposed task is simply too demanding to be carried beyond a certain elementary level of study. In some European universities it used to be called 'theological encyclopaedia', and on these terms, as the flood of information increased in volume, to master more than one field was seen to be a stark impossibility. Some scholars mastered more than others, but comprehensive knowledge was clearly impossible. At this point, a second approach, that generally labelled 'phenomenological' put in its appearance.

The phenomenological answer to the question of common ground, or (to use a slightly different expression) to what is universal, as opposed to what is local, variable and contingent, in religion, was *synchronic* rather than *diachronic*. It sought its answers, not in the historical *process*, but in the *function* of religion in the lives of individuals and communities, present as well as past. And in very many cases it came to place very great emphasis on the question of 'the holy' or 'the sacred' as the final key to understanding religious diversity.

But before we can ask whether this was and is a satisfactory answer, we must look briefly at one other attempt to grapple with this same question, that which won considerable support among European intellectuals toward the end of the eighteenth century, and which is commonly labelled 'Deism' (not to be confused with 'Theism', which means the belief in a personal God who is intimately concerned with the destiny of mankind: Deism lays the emphasis rather on the moral demands of a God who otherwise allows the world to function as best it can).

The Deists said, in effect, that by studying the world around him, man has been able to arrive at certain rational (and therefore universal) conclusions about the supernatural Power which created and which governs it. The world is basically orderly – witness the alternation of day and night, the seasons, the phases of the moon, the motions of the planets. These things could not have come about by chance; therefore there must be a Mind and a Will behind them. A Christian verse, first published in 1704, may serve to illustrate the point.

> The Spacious Firmament on high,
> With all the blue Ethereal Sky,
> And spangled Heav'ns, a Shining Frame,
> Their great Original proclaim.
> Th' unwearied Sun from Day to Day,
> Does his Creator's Power display,
> And publishes to every Land
> The Work of an Almighty Hand.
>
> Joseph Addison (1672-1719)

But beyond this, so the Deists held, the 'great Original' was, and is, in his nature moral: he has created not only a natural, but equally a moral order, to which humanity must conform. In creating man 'in his own image', he has provided man with a built-in moral compass of conscience, with the help of which he can tell right from wrong, and anticipate rewards and punishments for his good and bad deeds, if not in this life (though natural catastrophe could serve a punitive purpose), then certainly in the life to come. In principle this is a universal – and rational – moral law. The late eighteenth century called it 'natural religion', believing it to be found everywhere in the world where man had the capacity to reason, though inevitably overlaid by successive accretions, accidental misconceptions and deliberate distortions. Without going further into the byways of Deism, we can perhaps see that it at least provided scholarship with one means of bringing the world's religions together under a common canopy. All human beings have been created by the same God, and therefore all carry within them the same moral consciousness. True, each race and culture has found its own ingenious ways to break the moral law, and each has been able to build up its own ramshackle superstructure of myth, ritual, priestcraft, fear and superstition on the divinely-laid foundations. But the moral foundations had only been obscured, and not broken apart by these later developments. The purpose of the study of religion was therefore to lay bare the foundations, the eternal truth beneath and behind the accretions of centuries. Some religions might have more of this truth than others. Since the theory after all emerged from the Judaeo-Christian West, it was only natural that that composite tradition was considered to have a head start in this regard. In theory, Islam was not too far behind, but most Europeans were still rather afraid of Islam, and were reluctant to show it too much sympathy. But again in theory, all religions contained at least some moral truth, however slight, and this could be sought after and analysed.

In the long run, however, this solution to the problem of 'common ground' failed to maintain its position (though this is not to say that there may not be rationalists who still hold to some part of the theory). First, because it was optimistic about human rationality: in matters of religion, most believers do not reason in the same way as members of an Oxford Senior Common Room or the scholars of the Sorbonne. It is not a matter of whether religious believers 'think straight', but on what premises they actually *begin* to think. Closer knowledge of the religions of the world, past and present, failed to provide any very convincing proof that any religious tradition had actually begun along the lines suggested by the Deists, though most had, once a certain point had been passed, an admirably logical attitude to the riddle of the universe. On the contrary, what on fresh examination appeared to be genuinely universal in world religion was not the initial drawing of rational conclusions from the contemplation of the natural order, but rather an instinctive and emotional response to a massive and impenetrable mystery. Even before the eighteenth century was out, David Hume in Scotland and Friedrich Schleiermacher in Germany were urging that religion rests, not on foundations of cool moral calculation, but on something still more fundamental, namely fear of, and at the same time a sense of dependence upon, the powers that inhabit (or are imagined to inhabit) the unseen world. In a word, what was central, essential, universal in religion – and thus that which was therefore the most capable of being studied on a world map – seemed now to be not its *natural* and rational, but its *supernatural* and irrational component. One might go even further, and say that in Roman terms, where *religio* and *superstitio* come into contention, on this view it is *superstitio* which is the more 'universal' of the two, as well as being the more deserving of being called 'natural religion'. The Deists' 'natural religion' on the other hand was never more than an abstraction and an intellectual construction. (For further discussion, see Sharpe, 1978.)

Returning now to our original question: what is the common core of 'religiosity' in all the world's religious traditions? – by fairly common consent, when an answer is attempted, it usually centres on whatever the inquirer happens to regard as the heart of 'true' religion – usually either 'spiritual experience' or moral intensity, or both in combination. Writers speak of the 'golden core' of religion, the 'perennial philosophy', mankind's 'spiritual quest' and the like. Interestingly enough, though, they almost always succeed in conveying the impression that this quest is somehow to be pursued *in spite of* the outward ritual and organisational forms which religion takes, and that like mysticism (whatever that may be taken to mean), true knowledge of the innermost nature of religion is never likely to be either sought or understood by the average believer. It is perhaps a little odd to observe how often an apparently profound concern for the 'golden core' of religion seems to go hand in hand with a fair degree of contempt for the wood out of which pews are made, and for the day-to-day concerns of ordinary believers.

This is in my view a matter intimately related to the definition question which was discussed in the previous chapter. A certain kind of observer looks at a complex pattern of interrelated expressions of belief and belonging, but often sees only those which he is prepared to see (or which he is capable of seeing). That part which falls within his field of vision and meets with his approval *is* religion, and he loses no time in telling the world so – and incidentally, in consigning to the outer darkness all that does not meet with his approval. Equally, that part must be common to all religions worthy of the name, though probably likewise hidden under layers of exotic garbage. All the rest (and there may be a great deal of it) can then be happily dismissed, or left for the folklorists and anthropologists to study as and when the fancy takes them.

But is not the most readily observable, and demonstrably the most common, aspect of religion that with which we began this chapter – namely, the fact that believers subject considerable areas of their world to scales of value, according to their degree of 'holiness' or 'sacredness'? And that these persons, places, objects, times and seasons are, so to speak, rendered 'holy' or 'sacred' by association with some non-worldly source, or perhaps with one another, by contagion? I say that *believers* react in this way. However, I do not propose here and now to set limits to who is actually a believer, or to what it is that produces belief. Nor shall I enter into the question of what happens to 'desacralise' some of these things; but let me at least suggest that even where it has become inappropriate to speak of religion, there may remain a residual 'sacredness' in some areas (perhaps most notably political ideology and sport) which is capable of surviving even when every supernatural point of reference has vanished.

The trouble with words like 'holy' and 'holiness' is that they have been bandied about for many years, and that they have taken on as a result many associations and overtones, not all of which are helpful. (To call someone a 'holy Joe' or to characterise an attitude as 'holier than thou' is in neither case meant, or understood, other than as an insult.) 'Sacred', on the other hand, has been used rather less, and has deteriorated less. But either may be used in a pejorative sense: to 'holy Joe' we may add 'sacred cow', without further explanation. In these expressions what is conveyed is a sense of artificiality and insincerity. The trouble is, that the word 'holy' has in the course of time come to be associated only with *moral* qualities; and since it is widely assumed that one ought not to parade whatever moral excellences one might perchance have, aggressive self-righteousness on the one hand, and inexplicable withdrawal from normality on the other, is implied wherever the word is used. And yet when Hindus call a *sadhu* or a *sannyasin* a 'holy man' these moral associations remain in abeyance; nor are they even remotely in evidence when the Aboriginal people of Australia speak of their 'sacred sites': on the contrary, the matter is then treated (and not only by Aborigines) with the utmost seriousness.

I spoke a little earlier of a theory of the universal in religion, connected initially with the names of Hume and Schleiermacher. Neither, to the best of my knowledge, made much use of the interchangeable words 'holy' and 'sacred' in the elaboration of their theories. But in the years around the turn of the present century (scholars in the intervening years having been too obsessed with the ideas of evolution, progress and history to give much attention to anything else) Schleiermacher in particular was rediscovered – not disinterred merely, but brought back to life and made the focus of a new mode of looking at the world of religion. In 1899, Schleiermacher's most influential work *Ueber die Religion: Reden an die Gebildeten unter ihren Verachtern* [*Concerning Religion: Speeches to its Educated Despisers*], 1799, was reissued to mark the centenary of its first publication, with an introduction and postscript by Rudolf Otto, then a lecturer in the University of Göttingen. And there, in a manner of speaking, a connection was made: modestly at first, but with growing force, Schleiermacher's vision of religion as consisting essentially not in creeds or codes, not in rational conclusions about the nature of God, but in immediate experience of the Other, was launched by Otto and others into the world of scholarship, and increasingly into the world of religion on both the academic and the practical levels.

As a scholarly theory, this might still be of no more than peripheral antiquarian interest. And certainly Otto's later book *Das Heilige*, 1917 [*E. tr. The Idea of the Holy*, 1923] seemed to some critics to be old theology wearing a new hat. But something important had happened nevertheless. The rationalists had been banished from the sanctuary. Instead, it was now possible to claim, almost for the first time in modern intellectual history, that that which set 'religion' apart from 'non-religion' was the experience of the sacred, or the holy. Almost simultaneously, the French sociologists were also drawing attention to this same all-important distinction between 'sacred' and 'profane'.

But Otto on the German side, and Durkheim on the French, though they were using similar language, were not saying precisely the same thing. Otto was saying to his readers: think back to a particular kind of emotional experience which you may have had (and if you have never had such an experience, there is little point in your reading my book), in which you have found yourself confronted by an inexplicable Something, which had frightened you and attracted you at one and the same time. This Something is not a reflection of yourself, and the experience it produces in you is totally and qualitatively different from anything else you may have felt in any other situation. You probably have no name to give it; but since the ancient Latin name for Deity is *numen*, I will suggest, without trying to set bounds to whatever may have caused the experience to well up inside you, that you label the experience itself 'numinous' (on the analogy of omen and ominous). Concerning what may have actually *caused* the experience, opinions may differ – and in the long run, there were not lacking voices who said that what Otto was describing was certainly an experience of a sort, but that he offered no evidence of any kind to prove that the initial impulse came from outside the subject's mind; but Otto for his part was convinced that experiences of this peculiar, 'numinous' kind are clear enough evidence of the *Numen* (God) who produces them.

At virtually the same time, the French sociologist Emile Durkheim (an atheist of Jewish extraction, a fact which it would be as well to bear in mind when trying to relate him to the liberal Lutheran Otto) was also paying a good deal of attention to the distinction in human affairs between 'sacred' and 'profane', and was saying, in effect, that that which is especially valuable to a given community – a temple, a centre from which law proceeds, a charismatic leader, and so on – is protected from criticism and destruction by being placed in a special category. Were this not to take place, the community would be in danger, since it would then have no fixed points around which to construct its common life. This special category is the category of the 'sacred' (which is of course the precise equivalent of 'holy', the former word being derived from Latin and the latter from German), and all that is not 'sacred' is 'profane' (*pro fanum* = outside the sanctuary). Durkheim by no means denied the significance of the sacred; on the contrary, he affirmed its extreme importance. But whereas in Otto's view it began as a reflection of the Being of God, in Durkheim's, it amounted to no more than a reflection of the self-understanding of a human community, since that which is sacred becomes so by human consensus, and is preserved by immutable and (within certain limits) unalterable custom.

One might perhaps want to claim that the only value of these theories today is the insight which each provides into the mind of the period immediately preceding the First World War; but to my mind, their significance is not limited to whatever place they may occupy in the history of twentieth-century ideas.

If we take Otto's and Durkheim's positions as types and patterns, then it would not be too much to claim that they represent the two opposite poles of religious studies today – Otto pious, individual-centred, taking the data of religious studies as proof that God has never left himself without a witness; Durkheim rationalist, community-centred, taking precisely the same data as evidence that mankind's religiosity stems from his own and (particularly) his community's needs. Durkheim's is the 'mirror theory' of religion; Otto's the 'window theory' (these we shall discuss more fully in our next chapter). And as usual, we are forced to confess that the data as we have them will bear either interpretation.

And yet from the student's point of view, we are left with the phenomenon, not of 'the holy' or 'the sacred' (abstract nouns made out of adjectives are commonly words without substance), but of a variety of phenomena to which the words 'holy' and 'sacred' are capable of being attached. Otto and Durkheim, not to mention hosts of later writers, were concerned to put forward some theory of how the usage *originated*; these days we are less interested in questions of origin, and more in questions of function. Here a third witness may be called in.

Walter Baetke was a German scholar specialising in matters Nordic, much of whose work was published during the Nazi period in Germany, and who at least contrived to keep his work on a footing acceptable to the political eccentrics of his day and age (whether or not he was himself politically contaminated is in this connection neither here nor there). In 1942 he published a book, *Das Heilige im Germanischen* [*The Holy in Germanic Studies:* it has never been translated into English], which was both anti-Otto and opposed to the kind of evolutionary optimism to which Otto's brand of study so easily lent itself. One may say, forty years on, that Baetke was unnecessarily hard on Otto; but at least he had one solidly positive contribution to make to the 'holiness' discussion.

Briefly, Baetke took Otto to task for turning religion into psychology – and bad psychology at that. What does it prove, that a man may have had 'numinous' experiences? It may prove anything and nothing about the mind of man, but as a proof that there is a *numen* producing these experiences, it is worthless. From the religious point of view, one must start, not with the reactions of the subject (the believer), but with the characteristics of that in which faith, or trust, is placed (the supernatural).

What Baetke is here saying is that in human religious experience, people, places and things are not classified as 'holy' because of the feelings they arouse in us, but because they relate directly to a parallel order of divine being, a supernatural world which touches the world of common human experience at various points. It is a powerful world; but power is not its main category. The 'beings' who inhabit it exercise influence on the normal world, and make demands; but holiness is not exclusively a moral category. Its only characteristic is that it *exists* (or rather, that it is *believed* to exist); and in whatever ways it impinges upon human life, there will be a phenomenon which we may call 'holy'.

If the supernatural world did not communciate at all, then there would be absolutely no reason to regard anything as holy, that is, as qualitatively different from anything else. And that is part of the dilemma in which the modern Western student is so often placed: the process of secularisation (to which we shall return in due course) has already gone so far that in very many cases literally nothing is sacred. The category of the supernatural has practically ceased to exist, either because the supernatural has been effectively dismissed from most people's minds, or because if it exists at all, its expresses itself only in and through the everyday. A priest or minister is only a person who exercises particular functions, a church is only a building in which people meet from time to time (and which can be painlessly transformed into a museum, a theatre or a warehouse, should the occasion arise), the Bible is just another unread book.

But this should not be taken without more ado to mean that modern western society has absolutely no notion of the holy. As Acquaviva has said: 'Even though modern society appears to be becoming increasingly impoverished with respect to the phenomenal component of religion, ... none the less we cannot with certainty presuppose an impoverishment *tout court* of the sacred ...' (Acquaviva, 1979: 199). We must suspect, however, that rejection (or suppression, or failure to acknowledge) the element of the holy in one's own life is very likely to lead to the failure to recognise it in the lives of others. Aboriginal sacred sites in Australia are thoughtlessly made into tourist attractions or uranium mines; sacred carvings from Africa or Papua New Guinea become ornaments, as do Orthodox icons (than which there is nothing more sacred). A Swedish relative was genuinely surprised, on a recent visit to Sri Lanka, to be told that her new summer dress offended people, because its pattern was one of lotus blossoms, a symbol of the Buddha. The very title of 'Jesus Christ Superstar' caused untold distress to many Christians, for reasons which the young people who actually took part in the show were probably entirely unable to comprehend, since their lives no longer affirmed the particular sacred symbol which to the practising Christian is summed up in the name of Jesus Christ. To the orthodox Hindu, the most evocative of whose sacred symbols is the cow, cow-protection is a matter of primary importance, and the thought of non-Hindus actually eating beef is a well-nigh insuperable barrier to open communication. Such examples might be multiplied.

It might therefore be claimed without much exaggeration, and without necessarily endorsing any of the theories we have been examining, that *the study of religion is first and foremost a matter of learning to recognise and respect what is (or has been) holy in the lives of individuals and communities*. The study does not end there; but unless it begins there, it is unlikely to begin at all.

How, though, is one to begin to identify and respect the holy, unless one has already learned to recognise it in one's own life and the life of the community to which one belongs? Questions of this general kind have been asked repeatedly by students of religion, though often they make use of analogies to press home the point. Perhaps the commonest of these (as we have seen) is to compare the understanding of religion to the understanding of music. On the individual level, it may be argued that unless one has some 'religious experience' of one's own, one is as unable to understand the depths and heights of religion as a deaf man is to understand a Beethoven piano sonata. If one's ear is physically unable to capture the sounds, appreciation cannot even begin; there is an insuperable barrier to understanding. A deaf man could however 'explain' a piano sonata in a fashion, in terms of the wood, wire and ivory out of which the piano is made, the movements of the pianist's fingers and feet, and the mechanical processes which take place inside the instrument – all of which are accessible to anyone who takes the trouble to look. And the explanation would be a 'true' one, as far as it went; every statement would be verifiably accurate, measurable and repeatable – ideal material for scientific investigation. All that would be missing would be the music, passing along the line of communication from composer, through performer, to listener.

There are students of religion who seem to set about their task in very much this way, describing rituals element by element, producing statistics of belonging and attendance, carrying out minute verbal analysis of the contents of Scripture, but apparently being unable or unwilling to try to judge religion as what it always claims to be – a mode of communication with an ultimate reality which is not capable of being subsumed under purely this-worldly, sensory categories. The notion of the holy, or sacred, can in fact be dealt with in this way. In the Germany of the 1930s and 1940s the Nazis made much of a concept of *das Heilige* in respect of the nation, the party and the *Führer*; twenty years earlier, the school of Durkheim had argued that every society 'sanctifies' its own symbols, and virtually ends by worshipping itself. In each case, presuppositions were at work to prevent the acknowledgment of any order of Being outside the visible, measurable universe. And again, the explanations were plausible enough, as far as they went.

We do not at this point need to try to settle the question whether mankind's sacred symbols are, or are not, produced in response to an Ultimate Reality, or whether they are self-generated. All that we need to do here is to affirm their existence, to recognise that religious life depends upon them, and to try to place ourselves in the position of the person to whose life they give coherence and meaning. But again it is necessary to say that the secularised Westerner, whose symbols of value are few and ephemeral, may not find this a particularly easy task. Wilfred Cantwell Smith once expressed the difficulty in a nutshell when he wrote that '[t]he Hindu does not reverence the cow we see, but the cow he sees.' One is tempted to produce other versions of this epigram: 'The Muslim does not reverence the Koran we read, but the Koran he reads.' 'A rock called

Uluru is sacred to the Pitjandjara; Ayers Rock (its Australian name) is a tourist attraction.'

S.S. Acquaviva has written that 'the history of religion tells us where to find the sacred and allows us to grasp the state of mind, the psychological, psychosocial, and cultural realities within which the sacred patterns themselves are expressed. In a word, it throws into relief the bonds between personality structure and the experience of the sacred' (1979: 18). Perhaps we should rather say that at its best, the study of religion (not the history of religion merely) is capable of opening up these perspectives. It does not do so automatically, however, and much will always depend on the receptivity of the student. It might not be too wide of the mark to suggest that one of the first requirements of the competent student of religion is that he should attempt to grasp what, in human life, is sacred (or holy) to whom, and why. He must recognise that a very ordinary object or a very unremarkable person may be a focus of the sacred, for reasons which pass far beyond what can be immediately observed, and which are transmitted along the deep channels of tradition. Above all, he must be prepared always to approach this dimension of human life with sympathy where sympathy is possible, and even where it is not, with courtesy and respect. As Max Warren once put it, 'Our first task in approaching another people, another culture, another religion, is to take off our shoes, for the place we are approaching is holy. Else we may find ourselves treading on men's dreams.'

Five

The Supernatural and the Transcendent

Although it is not necessarily belief in the 'holiness' or 'sacredness' of persons, places, times and seasons that *makes* religion, we might at least claim that such a belief is one of the most widespread *signs* of religion. Söderblom's epigram: 'religious is the man to whom something is holy', is too sweeping a statement; but on the other hand it is certainly (or very probably) true that the man to whom nothing is holy is very probably irreligious. Further, we have seen that the 'holiness' question is not a very good point of entry into the matter of the origin of religion, since it generally places too much emphasis on the state of mind of the believer, and leaves open the very real possibility that the whole business centres on feeling-states. Now we must carry the argument a step further.

Whatever the critical observer may say or think, *to the believer* things are 'holy' or 'sacred' because they are points of contact between an unseen and the seen world, instruments of revelation, sources of information, determinants of destiny and the like; or else they are associated in some way with these things. But they are not believed to be such because they transmit impersonal 'power': rather because they are linked directly with another, parallel universe, an alternative order of being.

How the student reacts to all this will depend, as we have already said, on his or her spiritual and intellectual presuppositions. Believer and non-believer, 'insider' and 'outsider', look at precisely the same phenomena, and may up to a point enjoy similar experiences, but in the end arrive at totally different interpretations of their meaning and source. This has very little to do with the ways in which religion is organised in our Western world. Whatever we may say about 'religious experience' it is fairly clear that it is no respecter of denominational differences (as Christian charismatics are in process of discovering). Latterday impatience with the inherited forms of religion in Western society may be generated more by a *Zeitgeist* than by deep reflection; but although sometimes irritating in its facile blanket condemnations of 'the religious establishment', it has at least helped to cure some old misconceptions and break down some age-old barriers, namely those which limited 'religion' to the insights (and the errors) of only one stream of tradition. Today, 'the holy' may be assumed to be discoverable anywhere and everywhere, and if a sense of reverence is one of its signs, then it may be linked in diverse ways with manifestations as different as Jesus Christ (certainly historical), Castaneda's Don Juan (probably fictitious) and J.R.R. Tolkein's Gandalf (completely fictitious).

At the same time, it would be absurd to claim that experiences of the holy are universal, or even that those who have them, always relate them consciously to a supernatural, or transcendent order. It is simply silly to claim that, let us say, a 'Tolkien society' is 'a religion': true, it may have some of the marks of a religious community, particularly on the myth and ritual side; but it is always well enough aware that its Prophet has consciously created a fictitious world peopled by non-existent heroes and villains. From this world there may be lessons to be learned (and it is worth bearing in mind that much of what it contains is only slightly modified Germanic mythology); but it is artificial for all that, and there is never even the slightest suggestion that 'Gandalf saves' or that Tolkien's map of Middle Earth is to be regarded as a *cultic* (as opposed to an *allegorical*) map of the universe as individuals and communities experience it.

The 'religious' position, then, is not merely one in which holiness is attached to random phenomena, or located within an imaginary universe, but one in which holiness is accepted as part of the total, given universe in which individuals and communities live. It is not one in which unanswerable questions are raised, but in which questions are believed to have found their answers. It implies the existence of an unseen, though deeply felt, order of being beyond the range of mortality, an order which is pre-existent, supra-existent and post-existent.

There is a celebrated passage in Bede's *History of the British Church and People* in which, faced with the choice between an old form of religion and a new, Christian, form, an anonymous *thegn* at the table of King Edwin of Northumbria compares the life of man to the flight of a sparrow through a warm banqueting-hall on a winter's night.

The bird comes out of the darkness, flies for a few brief moments through the light, and then disappears into the darkness again. Such (he says) is the life of man: and if this new faith is able to tell us anything about the earlier and the later darkness, then it ought at least to be given the chance to prove itself.

The matter could not be put more starkly. However many difficulties may accompany life on earth, and however passionately men may scratch for their daily bread and swing their little banners while on earth, the ultimate questions will not be silenced. *That* things happen anyone can see; *why* things happen, and *where* the process is leading – and *who* is finally in control – are the fundamental religious questions. The 'religious' answer always relates to a power or powers beyond this world; other answers are possible, and common enough, but whatever else they may be, if they lack the element of the supernatural or the transcendent, they are not religious.

But again we are brought up against the question: but what if there is no supernatural to relate to, and what if this 'transcendent' is no more than a projection of man's longing for the unattainable? This is a question which the student may sidestep, but which will often try to ambush him. As always, two sets of equally satisfactory (and equally unsatisfactory) answers are possible.

The sceptical answer begins as a rule by assuming that there is no order of being other than that which communicates itself to us through our senses. To be sure, it will admit, the senses are imperfect instruments, but respond to stimuli and still more to deliberate training. The hands of a navvy, the hands of a concert pianist, and the hands of a brain surgeon are all hands, and the only difference between them is that they have been trained to respond differently to what the brain tells them to do. Brains are incredibly capacious computing mechanisms, but cannot react to what they do not know. Early man (in the Palaeolithic age, say) could react only in fear and apprehension to the unknown – that is to say, to almost everything beyond the range of a few physical functions. Some explanation of the rest he had to find for himself, partly on the basis of what he could observe, partly backed up by mental short-circuits and distortions in dreams, trances and the like (probably brought on in part by under-nourishment, disease and poisoning). But at this stage man had no way of distinguishing between types of experience, and no possibility of understanding their physical causes; while in respect of the actual world around him, he had to quieten his curiosity and moderate his very natural fears as best he could. Though conscious of little else, he was conscious of the struggle for existence. On the one side there were the inexplicable powers which gave him what he needed to support life – food, water, sunshine, shelter. On the other there were the still more inexplicable powers which were trying to take life from him. Knowing nothing of bacilli and their connection with disease, he postulated 'loss of soul' as its cause and supported shamans to retrieve the soul from the regions beyond. Knowing nothing of thunderstorms, he postulated a Thor in the sky, beating a drum and throwing a hammer. The desert he peopled with demons, the forest with trolls, the sea with incredible monstrosities. Worst of all was his fear in face of death, and concerning whatever lay beyond the grave, his imagination knew no bounds.

But gradually, the clouds begin to lift. The more man learns, the more 'supernatural' occurrences turn out to have a 'natural' explanation, and the more the old imaginings take on the appearance of childish fantasies. Religious traditions are tenacious, and often ignore, or try to explain away, the new knowledge. But more and more priests have to abandon their sanctuaries and leave room for the scientifically enlightened – the psychologists, sociologists, anthropologists and the rest, who assure us either that religion is no more than an assemblage of fantasies from the childhood of the human race, or that if it is to survive, it must be on other terms than those with which it began. For despite everything, there remains morality, and religion may have some positive value if it can persuade people to treat one another with consideration, make them reliable workers, and help prevent war (though in this last area it is usually added that its record has not been of the best).

On this view, then, 'the transcendent' is at worst purely imaginary, and positively harmful if it persuades people to stop thinking. At best, it is a desire for improvement beyond the bounds of what is currently experienced. To opt for the term 'supernatural' makes matters still worse. On this view there *is* no supernatural, and the study of religion becomes what Freud believed it to be, namely an inquiry into pathology, neurosis and illusion.

The 'believer' is not deterred by these arguments, however. Arch-conservatives aside, most Christians (to speak only of the group I know best) are these days prepared to accept most of what yesterday's radicals wrote and said. Of course mankind has grown, and of course the mind of man has evolved from deplorable beginnings. But although many are nervous when confronted with the word 'supernatural' (mainly because they are afraid to set too firm limits to what we may regard as 'natural'), 'the transcendent' remains an acceptable option – though whether because of, or in spite of its conceptual vagueness it is sometimes hard to say. They point out, however, that the mind of man, whatever may have been its failings, has always wanted to pass beyond its limitations and those of the body to which it is attached. Is it possible, they ask, that this could have happened, had the passing world actually been an end in itself? Is not the belief in evolution a modern mythology, supported only in part by the available evidence? And does it not involve a remarkable degree of faith – though a faith not in a creative Mind, but in the power of matter to generate and shape itself in no one's image in particular? While concerning our ancestors' attempts to explain the battle of life and death in dramatic terms, and their capacity to shape myths, these faculties are alive and well, and flourishing in the last quarter of the twentieth century, though usually under the label of 'politics' rather than 'religion'. As their trump card, they produce the fact of death, and point out that there at least is a dimension of transcendence which none of us can avoid, and about which none of us knows anything whatsoever. And suddenly we find ourselves back in seventh-century Northumbria, watching the flight of a sparrow through a leaky, draughty, smoky wooden building, and straining our eyes to peer into the darkness outside, wondering whether God, Grendel or a gaping void is waiting to receive us.

The result is deadlock. Neither side is prepared to accept the other's point of view. The supernatural either exists or it does not; there is either a transcendent order (or at least a limit to the present order, with 'something' on the other side) or there is not. The facts of the human case are capable of being interpreted in either way. Crudely, we might call the former (that of the rationalist materialists), the 'mirror theory', the latter the 'window theory'.

According to the mirror theory, in the so-called supernatural or transcendent, the observer sees only a reflection of himself: not a true reflection, for in the best of mirrors, images are reversed, and this is not the best of mirrors. Divine power is human power writ large, and omnipotence the worst of all power-worlds. Divine love likewise: boundless human love of the kind we all crave but find only fitfully and fleetingly. Small wonder, then, that between Euhemeros and von Däniken many attempts have been made to show, not merely that divine qualities are inflated human qualities, but that the gods themselves once lived and died (or at least disappeared into Outer Space) as we do.

The window theory, on the other hand, allows to the mind a *transmissive* function. Orthodox believers take some such view more or less for granted, without always being able to speak of it in this way. Aming the less orthodox, the names of Emanual Swedenborg, William James and Henry David Thoreau will serve as examples of those who have held the mind, under certain conditions, to be capable of receiving 'influxes' from the world of pure spirit. Spiritualists might be expected to believe it, though in practice the spirit world appears to possess a devastating triviality, which few are able to explain. Every clairvoyant believes it, and many who would die rather than admit it suspect that there may be some such mystery hidden at the heart of the universe. But for most, it remains only a suspicion, since institutional religion (within which most believers after all belong) tends, and has always tended, to find direct communications from the supernatural order uncomfortable and sometimes dangerous.

There is a third possibility, namely that the barrier between the seen and the unseen worlds may have the nature of a two-way mirror. This may perhaps be called the agnostic alternative. The transcendent (if there is a transcendent) can see us, doubtless to its infinite sorrow; but from our side, we can see only ourselves, and whether there is, or is not anyone on the other side, we shall never know.

Students of religion inevitably occupy one or other of these positions, and accept one or other of these theories, whether consciously or not. But over and above these alternatives, there is the further complicating factor that on the side of the 'window theory', there are, so to speak, windows of different shapes and sizes, some of them plain, some filled with ecclesiastical stained glass, and most of them pointing in only one direction, depending on where the architects have at some time in the past placed them. The illustration must not become too elaborate, but the general point is that in religion as a focus of belief and practice, though the existence of the supernatural is postulated and accepted, what is believed about it is limited by the size and shape of the window through which the light comes, that is, by the nature of the culture within which belief is sustained. At times, however, even stained-glass windows can be broken and walls knocked down (not that they *should* be, for they serve other functions: but they *may* be, in times of reformation and revolution); and when this happens, even the oldest traditions may change.

It may be the hardest thing in the world for the student who is privately convinced of the non-existence of a supernatural order, not to superimpose this conviction upon the beliefs of others, by saying (or thinking) that whatever those 'others' may seem to believe, or claim to believe, since there is no supernatural to relate to, their beliefs must be illusory, and rest on other foundations entirely than those of the response to revelation which they claim to be. Things are not made any the easier by the fact that Western, and other, rationalists have so often in the past done precisely that, and have produced explanation after explanation, designed to explain away religion, its origins and its development, as a product of an immature or a diseased human mind.

Of course, convictions are convictions, and no amount of arguing will accomplish more than a rise in blood-pressure on the part of the one who feels threatened by alternative point of view – which, if it be 'true', could make all the difference in the world (and perhaps beyond it) to so much of life. But at least the student must learn, however difficult it may be at first, to accept that *when believers say that there is an alternative, parallel order of being to the things of this world, they mean precisely what they say*, and shape their lives accordingly. It matters little whether this order be called supernatural, supernormal or transcendent. But it matters very greatly that it is assumed actually to exist, that it communicates with mankind (though not constantly or in every situation), and that it implicitly affects human life at every turn. That modern Westerners have found ingenious ways to ignore, or even to deny the existence of, a supernatural order while still claiming to be 'religious' is another matter entirely, a reaction born of the interplay of secularisation and commitment to communities and their values. It need not for the moment concern us. But the semi-secularised Westerner must at least accept that he is something of an oddity in world history, and that to understand either the past or the non-secular present, he must at least attempt to enter into a world of values and presuppositions which he must try to understand, even when his understanding must stop short of commitment. Goethe once wrote that 'Wer der Dichter will verstehen, muss in Dichters Lande gehen' – to understand the poet, it is necessary to enter his country. Precisely the same is true of the religious believer.

What of this 'supernatural order'? In what does it consist? Here again, two answers are possible. Either that it is impossible to speak of it in human language, in which case the only possibility is silence – the final point of 'mysticism'; or that it can be described by analogy (in images and symbols) and in relation to its direct influence on human life. The former we may call a *via negativa*, a way of non-affirmation; the latter a *via positiva*, a way of affirmation which, though it may sometimes stop short of claiming to know what transcendence actually is, believes that it expresses itself in symbols, myths, and images which can be comprehended, given the right key.

Here again we are faced with a serious problem of understanding, since the language of myths and symbols is not a timeless language, but very much bound up with whatever conditions obtain in specific places on the earth's surface and at specific times in its history. In an age of atomic warfare, swords, suits of armour and boar's-head helmets are no longer compelling symbols of anything except remote barbarism; fire, water, sun and moon, on the other hand, are still capable of carrying a symbolical, as well as a physical, meaning. When a few years ago Rudolf Bultmann announced that, to be understood in the twentieth century, the message of the New Testament would have to be 'de-mythologised', that is, set free from the images and symbols which belonged to the first, but not to the twentieth, century, he believed that he was doing religion a great service. What he did not grasp was the extent to which, in Christianity as in other parallel cases, the supernatural/transcendent can be expressed only through groups of interrelated symbols, and that to free the message from the medium in which it expresses itself is an option open only to a very few intellectuals, accustomed to thinking in terms of moral diagrams and conceptual abstractions.

To think in symbols, by association rather than according to the conventions of cause and effect, has at various times been characterised as 'prelogical' (by Lévy-Bruhl, before his final change of heart), 'subconscious' (by Carl Gustrav Jung) and 'archaic' (by

Mircea Eliade). We may call it what we will, but what it amounts to is man's belief that he lives in a world filled with symbols of the holy, tangible signs of the presence in human life of beings who do not die (or who, having died, live on in another dimension), whose power is not limited as human power is limited by the contingencies of time and space, *and who in some way hold human destiny in their hands.*

It is perhaps this last point which more than any other separates 'archaic' belief in the supernatural from 'modern' belief in the transcendent. Both set limits to the rough-and-ready workings of the untutored human mind; but whereas the more modern view claims in effect that there are undiscovered dimensions to the human mind itself, and that the mind is capable of being expanded so as to exercise power over its environment on its own account, the archaic view is that of an *external* constellation of power which the mind cannot create, but to which it can and must relate. To be sure, many archaic (and some modern) philosophies claim that within man there is that which belongs essentially to the supernatural order – a soul, spirit, *atman*, or divine spark, which has in some way become imprisoned in a mortal body, and which, if it is to be true to its own nature, has to strive for liberation from the limits imposed upon it by crude perishable matter. But leaving such speculations on one side, the common human view is less that of an individual immortal soul imprisoned and seeking to be set free from a ramshackle prison of skin and bone than of a vast human company attempting to survive in a world ruled by an invisible government which metes out life, less as a 'human right' than as a privilege; and like all privileges, life is granted only on certain conditions.

The authority of the supernaturals derives first and foremost from an act of creation, in which the earth was made habitable (having previously existed 'waste and void', that is, as primeval chaos) and in which life's patterns were established in the alternation of day and night, heat and cold, seedtime and harvest and the rhythms of reproduction. Having been shaped, the cosmic pattern is maintained by immortals and mortals together, by the power of the immortals and the acknowledgment of that power by mortals in sacrifice, prayer, ritual and obedience to whatever laws the immortals may have made for the maintenance of the pattern. To the cosmic order of creation (leading inevitably to maturity, decline and destruction) there corresponds an identical human order, from birth and infancy to old age and death; this pattern, too, is established and maintained by the 'determiners of destiny' and needs to be acknowledged at every critical point. As with individuals, so with social units, family, tribe and nation: each is governed from beyond itself, and depends for its well-being on the way or ways in which it relates to those in whose hands ultimate power lies.

The question now is not whether this is a view of the universe which is acceptable to the Western world of the 1980s. Clearly for the most part it is not. But unless the student grasps that 'presecular' man actually based all his reasoning about the universe on some local variant of this cosmic pattern, and acted accordingly, full understanding of archaic religion is bound to prove elusive, if not entirely inaccessible.

Because on this view, the natural and the supernatural worlds intersect at many points, and because at each of those points there are tangible symbols of the effect of the supernatural order on the natural, archaic man's world is full of signs of the supernatural – times, seasons, sites, edifices, artefacts, sounds, animals, persons – none of which has been selected at random, but all of which have been 'sanctified' (made holy) by association. Of course they may be important to a community, though as a rule communities grow around them, rather than create them deliberately. Of course they may inspire the kind of feeling that Rudolf Otto labelled 'the sense of the numinous', but it is not there that their importance lies. Their importance always rests in the accepted belief (which is maintained until something drastic happens to disturb it) that at that point there is a direct intersection between two orders of being, of which human feeling-states are at best only a pale reflection.

In the history of religion, belief in the supernatural is altogether more explicit than belief in the transcendent. The historian-phenomenologist can speak only of that which he observes, either in the records of the past or in the religious life which he sees around him; and what he observes is a process in which the dramatically explicit becomes, or appears to become, vaguer and less definite as time passes. I shall try to explain more fully what I mean.

In 'archaic' societies, the supernatural world is in many ways comparable with human society. It is in the first place a hierarchy of power. At the top of the ladder there is what scholars have generally come to call a 'high god' (in German, *Hochgott*), who is all-powerful, undying, incapable of being imagined in human form – though this does not prevent *at a later stage* the attempt being made to visualise him – and thought of in a general way as being located 'up there' or 'out there'. To say that he is 'located in the sky' or that he is a 'sky-god' is an oversimplification. Certainly we read in the Prophet Isaiah that '[i]t is he who sits above the circle of the earth, and its inhabitants are like grasshoppers; who stretches out the heavens like a curtain, and spreads them like a tent to dwell in' (40:22). Certainly he may be thought of as (and perhaps even called) 'the old man in the sky' by those who must have simple images at all costs. In the same chapter of Isaiah we read: 'To whom then will you liken God, or what likeness compare with him?' (v.18) – the point on this occasion being that man-made objects do not and cannot represent him; nor can human thought do so, save vaguely and by analogy. Isaiah would probably have thought even Michelangelo's ceiling in the Sistine Chapel frivolous and unworthy. But this is not to say that nothing can be known of him (and it might be as well to say at once that the masculine personal pronoun is no more adequate than other human devices where the 'high god' is concerned: 'he' may equally well, and equally improperly, be called 'she' or 'it'); what he has created can be observed; and at his command he has a vast host of subordinates.

It is at this point that the art (or rather, the imagination) of the myth-maker makes its contribution. A century ago, Friedrich Max Müller believed this to be the beginning of all religion's troubles; had man, he argued, been able to rest content with a single vision of the infinite, without surrounding it with a menagerie of imaginary subordinates, supernatural consorts, cabinet ministers, police chiefs, friends and relations, then the modern world would not have had to face the daunting task of clearing all this rubbish away in the interests of pure ethical religion. Be that as it may, it is certainly true that 'archaic' religion fills the space between mortal man and the ineffable high god with a hierarchy of supernatural power, in a chain of command reaching all the way down through gods and goddesses, archangels and angels, to the guardian spirits of well and tree, hearth and home, and the imps who curdle milk and give one toothache. Within the hierarchy there are beings male and being female, beings static and beings mobile, beings helpful and beings malicious. What they all have in common is that they owe their existence in one way or another to the high god, and that none of them is encased in a perishable envelope of flesh and blood and bones. To be sure, some of them have *been* human beings – from the

Christian saints at one extreme to 'ghosts' at the other – and throughout Western intellectual history there have been those who have sought to prove that the world of the supernaturals is made up entirely of the inflated memories of the once-living and the once-powerful. It contains such memories; but it contains so much besides that the 'euhemeristic' theory (after its apparent originator, the Greek Euhemeros) can never explain more than part of the evidence.

The 'archaic' supernatural world is therefore a hierarchy, similar in its structure to feudal human society (and therefore easily explained away by democratic moderns as a mere reflection of outworn social systems): in some respects an extension upward of the human aspect of 'the great chain of being', in others running parallel to it. At the lowest level of the supernatural hierarchy there are beings whose influence is limited to a tiny place or a minimal local function. The higher one ascends on the ladder the more widespread the influence becomes, for instance in respect of the supernaturals who control the space betwen 'heaven' and earth – deities of wind, storm, thunder and lightning, and the like. And at the very top of the ladder one passes into the regions of universality. Much the same might of course be said of the human feudal hierarchy, with its local, provincial, regional and universal governors. And the parallel aspect holds good at least in respect of those supernaturals with whom the individual is expected to maintain relationships. The peasant may *acknowledge* the king and *serve* the king; but no one expects that he will relate to the king, other than on very special occasions. Most of the time he relates to the king only through the subordinates whom the king's authority has appointed – the landlord, the local tax collector, and so on. Similarly there will be times when the man at the plough will come before the high god; but for most of the time his relations with the supernatural world will be limited to those lesser immortals who exercise direct influence on his workaday life, including those members of his own family who have passed through the vale of death.

But once the social pattern has been broken, the ancient sacred sites abandoned, the mounds and the graveyards desecrated, the springs and wells polluted or stopped up, what remains may be little more than a collection of stories out of an incomprehensible past. Perhaps the king still rules; his court, on the other hand, has disappeared for good.

The inadequacy of Western intellectual tradition to deal with this archaic pattern of religious belief is nowhere better illustrated than in respect of the words which it uses to try to describe the supernatural world and man's relations to it. Are, for instance, *all* the supernaturals 'gods' and 'goddesses', irrespective of their place in the hierarchy? Hindu India is generous, and is prepared to call almost any supernatural being a god or a goddess, and to allow the individual to relate to any of them in acts of 'worship'. Buddhism acknowledges them, but denies the right of any of them to be called self-existent or to be regarded as a supreme creator-god; the result is notoriously confusing to the Western mind, used to hard and fast categories of deity. The religions of the Semitic tradition – Judaism, Christianity and Islam in order of emergence – are known to be 'monotheistic', in that they acknowledge only one God (the high god of archaic belief in most respects), and forbid the worship of lesser supernaturals. But they do not forbid their acknowledgment. Angels, saints, spirits and demons are part of all three traditions, and are certainly not believed to be powerless; but they are not to be approached as one would approach God, and other words have been found to describe their acknowledgment, and limited, local intercessions directed in their direction. It seems that monotheistic theory has here set up pragmatic barriers (over a certain line, 'worship', below it, something else) which archaic and primal religion does not need and in many cases still cannot understand.

Even archaic religion was never capable of acknowledging or worshipping a multiplicity of high creator gods. It was, on the other hand, quite able to acknowledge a multitude of lesser supernaturals on the lower rungs of the ladder *differentiated by function*. To use a modern political analogy, for the citizen of a state to serve two or more kings or presidents is commonly regarded as treasonable; but he may, and indeed must, acknowledge the heads of half a dozen government departments, each at the proper time and in the appropriate situation. Most of the lesser gods of polytheistic belief are of this kind: they are officials, rather than heads of state (though this does not prevent some from becoming under certain circumstances heads of state). But this monotheists cannot and will not accept: having in the course of time learned to relate 'worship' only to the Supreme Being, others' acknowledgment of the authority of the lesser deities within their proper spheres is labelled 'worship' and condemned accordingly. Much more might be said, but one is left with the impression that there have arisen misunderstandings along the way, caused in part by carelessness in differentiating between different classes of supernatural beings on the mythological level, between their functions, and between the words which may be used to describe man's relationship to them.

With 'the transcendent' there are no such problems. The difficulty here is deciding what, if anything, the word actually means in positive terms. It implies something or other beyond the range of the individual's everyday capabilities and concerns; but what precisely? *Precisely*, the term 'the transcendent' means nothing at all, since it refers only to that which is transcended, and then only in a negative sense. One cannot relate to the transcendent; at most, one can look in the direction in which one believes that it is to be found. At worst to speak of the transcendent is modern man's way of speaking of the God in which he no longer believes in the old terms (as personal, omnipresent, omnipotent, and so on), but whom he is afraid to reject altogether. In this situation, to speak of belief in the transcendent is an oblique way of registering one's lack of belief in the finality of the temporal. At best, the language of the transcendent serves as an intellectual replacement for the language of a discredited supernatural, with all its mythological accretions. In this way the genuineness of the age-old religious impulse can be preserved, without committing oneself in any way to any particular shape which the supernatural might be believed to have taken. The ancient myths can then be interpreted as dramatic images of the transcendent, rituals as performances affirming the transcendent, 'holiness' itself as a mode of the transcendent.

The modern believer may well choose to speak in this non-committal way of that in which he believes, to say in effect that 'I feel there to be something out there, but I'm not sure what it is.' The student, on the other hand, unless he or she happens to be trying to get to grips with varieties of modern religiosity, has in most cases to come to terms with belief in a terribly explicit supernatural, with all its paradoxes and all the opportunities it provides for post-positivist intellectual snobbery. At least if one begins with the categories of the supernatural, one has the chance of comprehending the process by which it lost its shape and content, and became the ill-defined transcendent; to begin with the transcendent, on the other hand, may well make it impossible for the student ever to appreciate the supernatural, other than as an archaic curiosity. Some may want to claim that intellectual honesty permits only the latter course, and that all that is left of religion in our day is precisely this sense of the transcendent coupled with an awkward sense of moral obligation. But those who see the study of religion in this light will, I fear, never understand any form of religion save their own. And that surely is a pity.

Six

The One and the Many: Religion and Religions

The question with which we shall be concerned in this chapter has to do with the relationship between religion ('the one') and religions ('the many'). From the student's point of view, it tends to be formulated in this way: given the observable plurality of religious traditions in the world, how many 'religions' is it necessary to study, and for how long, before one can claim a thorough knowledge and understanding of 'religion'?

Most students of religion would agree that one ought not to paint on too narrow a canvas. A century ago, Friedrich Max Müller urged that in respect of religion (and much else), 'he who knows one, knows none', and that some degree of parallel study was absolutely necessary for anyone wanting to take the matter seriously. A similar point was being made at the same time by the followers of Charles Darwin and Herbert Spencer: that religion is the *genus* of which the individual religions are the *species*: no biologist would be satisfied for very long with the study of only one species, nor should the student of religion. As Allan Menzies put it in a book first published in 1895, 'What everyone with any interest in the subject is striving after, is a knowledge of the religions of the world not as isolated systems which, though having many points of resemblance, may yet, for all we know, be of separate and independent growth, but as connected with each other and as forming parts of one whole. *Our science, in fact, is seeking to grasp the religions of the world as manifestations of the religion of the world* [my italics] (Menzies, 1922: 5).

A few years later, however, the outstanding German historian of religion Adolf von Harnack was taking a quite different position, and saying in effect that this ideal may be all very well in theory, but that it is totally impossible to carry out in practice. On 3 August 1901 he delivered an address in the University of Berlin on 'The Task of the Theological Faculties and the General History of Religion', in which he stated that the theological student has all that he can possibly cope with in the serious study of Christianity. For an ill-equipped student who knows none of the relevant languages and is badly informed about cultural and historical backgrounds to wander around among the religions of the world is practically a waste of time, since it can give rise only to a habit of superficiality and dilettantism. Harnack's view was that unless a religion can be studied in detail, particularly through its sacred texts, it is better not to try to study it at all. These conditions can be met in the case of Christianity (or they could, in the Germany of 1901): in a faculty of theology, they cannot be met in respect of any other religion, and one ought not to try. Added to which, Harnack was of the opinion – against Max Müller – that comparison is unnecessary. In Christianity, the student has all that he can possibly need. Christianity *is* religion at its highest level of development, summing up and fulfilling every other religious manifestation that the world has ever seen. Why then waste time aiming for the impossible, when the possible is also the desirable?

In these days, given the choice between 'he who knows one, knows none' (Max Müller) and 'he who knows one – Christianity – knows all that he needs' (Harnack), it would be easy to assume that the former represents the religious studies (or comparative religion) alternative, while the latter belongs within the orbit of Christian theology. But this would not necessarily be correct. Harnack was for one thing not attempting to forbid or suppress the study of religions other than Christianity, but merely to say that a faculty of Christian theology was not the best place for it to be carried out. In a faculty of arts (or humanities), on the other hand, where the linguistic and other facilities for *thorough* study are available, the study of other religions and cultures was to be encouraged. Indirectly, he was saying something else as well.

His position in fact implied that 'comparative religion' can be pursued *within* Christianity. And this is undoubtedly true. Without spending further time in turn-of-the-century Berlin, may we not allow that there is under the umbrella of Christianity enough, and more than enough, material to support a lifetime of comparative study? For as Ernst Troeltsch pointed out over half a century ago, 'Christianity is itself a theoretical abstraction. It presents no historical uniformity, but displays a different character in every age ...' (Troeltsch, 1923: 13). He might have added that it displays even greater diversity in geographical perspective. There is Christianity as it is found in Europe (North and South), America (North and South), Africa, India, the Far East, South-East Asia, the Pacific. Among its personalities there are prophets, priests and kings, saints and sinners, mystics and mountebanks, politicians and prelates. There is every form of ritual, from Westminster Abbey to a Quaker meeting-house, from the Salvation Army to an *ashram* in South India. Around its frontiers cluster vast numbers of breakaway and reform movements, some well known, other totally obscure. At times it seems that the only feature which Christians have in common is the naming of Jesus Christ as Lord.

Of course there is absolutely no reason why one should limit observations of this kind of Christianity. Much the same might be said of all of today's 'world religions', each of which exhibits an almost infinite variety of personalities, sects, rituals, philosophies and attitudes. Hinduism is not only the metaphysical tradition of Shankara: it is equally the aestheticism we find in Rabindranath Tagore, the ethical intensity of Gandhi, the semi-westernised philosophy of Radhakrishnan, and the worship of the local mother-goddess in some obscure South Indian village. It is Rishikesh, Auroville and the Hindu Mahasabha. Perhaps, too, in some sense it is a company of western devotees of the Lord Krishna, cavorting around the huge statue of their god on the streets of Sydney. And who – anywhere in the world – can claim to have observed, recorded and explained all these diverse manifestations of what the textbooks insist is *one* religion called 'Hinduism'?

One could continue along these lines, but I trust that the point will have been made, that when Harnack spoke of one tradition, one religion, containing within itself all that the student needs for the purposes of comparative study, he was making a valid point.

And yet in many cases the point does not *seem* to be a valid one, perhaps because most people find it so hard to distinguish between an idealised (or caricatured) view of some religious tradition and the whole range of observable phenomena which that tradition embraces. The statement 'Christianity contains everything the student needs in order to be able to pursue comparative studies' is phenomenologically true. But it does not sound true to the student whose vision of Christianity is limited to what he or she may have discovered, and in many cases reacted against, on the local level. The impression is liable to be conveyed either that it is being claimed that Christianity contains all that is *worth* studying in the world of religion, or that behind the scenes is the vision of an idealised Christianity having only an incidental connection with the chapel or the church on the corner. And lest it should be thought that the choice of Christianity as an illustration should itself be weighted, precisely the same impression might well be created by the statement that Buddhism, or Hinduism, or Islam, contains all the material necessary for the purposes of comparative study. In these cases, too, there is a gap between these traditions as observable phenomena and what might be claimed to be their most fully perfected form or their idealised essence.

Most students of today simply assume, however, that a religion is what is subsumed under a text-book chapter and a particular heading. From time to time, arguments have been put forward to support this assumption. In the late 1930s, for instance, the Dutch scholar Hendrik Kraemer wrote:

> Every religion is a living, indivisible unity. Every part of it – a dogma, a rite, a myth, an institution, a cult – is so vitally related to the whole that it can never be understood in its real function, significance and tendency, as these occur in the reality of life, without keeping constantly in mind the vast and living unity of existential apprehension in which the part moves and has its being (Kraemer, 1938: 135).

But I am not sure that this is a true principle. Certainly there is a largely unconscious fashion which decrees that we should speak of each 'great religion' *as though* it were such a unity, and in some cases there is a vague unity of sentiment, or 'solidarity' between co-religionists, particularly when under pressure. But the closer one comes to the actualities, the less marked does the vision of 'totalities' become.

From the time in the eighteenth century when the scholars of the West started to divide up the religion of the world into the geographically and culturally determined religions of the world, and to label each as an '-ism' (Hinduism, Buddhism, Muhammadanism, Confucianism, Taoism, Shintoism and the rest) there has been created the habit of mind which all too lightly supposes that everything which the curious outsider is able to place under one or another of these labels, actually conforms to everything else under the same label. To be sure, it has always been possible to add some qualifying adjective – 'higher', 'lower', 'priestly', 'popular', 'mystical', or whatever – to indicate that there are after all differences within these '-isms'. And yet the qualifications have seldom made much impression on the massive (and misleading) simplicity of the basic classification system.

On the one hand, there has been the very real problem of understanding why believers belonging to two branches of ostensibly the same 'religion' actually appear to believe quite different things about God, the world, and man's place in it, and how they can go to such lengths to affirm their beliefs. (This is not, incidentally, a problem peculiar to Christianity, though Christian history has seen more than enough examples of theological pugnacity and what might be called the 'venomenology' of religion: Hindus and Muslims, too, have been known to behave in precisely similar ways.) And on the other, there has been the difficulty which has faced western scholars when they have discovered in other parts of the world believers who have apparently been happy to belong to two or three such 'religions' simultaneously. Here pre-revolutionary China is an excellent case in point. Although the western scholar usually wrote of 'the three religions of China' (Confucianism, Taoism, Buddhism), he was forced at the same time to admit that in some mysterious way, most Chinese were able to 'belong' to all three religions at one and the same time. To meet these and similar cases, there was introduced the category of 'syncretism' – how typical that it should have been yet another '-ism' – meaning an untidy muddle of elements drawn from more than one tradition at once. But always behind talk of syncretism there lies the assumption that religion is divided up into well-defined doctrinal and ritual systems, that normal human beings belong to only one of them at once, and that to give one's allegiance across the frontiers is tantamount to religious bigamy.

What, then, are the 'living' and 'indivisible' unities of which Kraemer spoke with such confidence? Do we not have some right to suspect that in many cases they are intellectual constructions, principles of lecture-room classification with the help of which the western rationalist scholar has tried to impose order on an otherwise chaotically multifaceted religious reality?

To be sure, what we are in the habit of calling 'the world's great religions' are more than random conglomerations of unrelated elements. Each has a notion of where the final seat of authority in religion is to be found: in holy scripture – the Bible, the Qur'an, the Veda – and sacred assembly; most have founder-prophets or founder-seers – Jesus, Muhammad, the Buddha; each has a history, an ethos, a 'tonality' of its own. And yet when all this has been acknowledged, and when every last ecumenical movement has been registered, there remains the unavoidable fact that over the years, every 'great religion' has been divided and subdivided many times, and that each subdivision has tended to build up a value-system of its own, based on teachings which may be startlingly at variance with those of other branches from the same religious stem.

The point at issue between them is not whether God (or whatever other name may be given to the ground of all being) exists, or whether knowledge of that ultimate Reality is accessible to mere mortals. On that level, religions have as a rule been able to find much common ground. The divisions within, as well as between, the systems arise at the point of *revelation* and *mediation*: how can we claim to know anything worth knowing about Ultimate Reality, and what are we to do in order to relate to it? Up to a certain point, chains of tradition may be fairly uniform; but once that point is passed, they are apt to part company.

Again taking Christianity as an example, the scriptures of the Old and New Testaments are the common property of all Christians, and the figure of Jesus Christ is the focal point of faith. But no Christian tradition actually stops there: superimposed on the authority of the Bible there is the additional authority of the results of a process of selection and interpretation, which in the course of time has created a motley collection of documents explanatory of the New Testament (which of course 'explains' the Old). Some are counted authoritative by numerically strong churches (The Augsburg Confession for Lutherans, the 39 Articles for Anglicans, the documents of various Councils for Roman Catholics). But the same function is filled by other documents in other cases: *The Book of Mormon, Science and Health with Key to the Scriptures* and even *The Mo Letters* (the interpretative 'scripture' of the Children of God). Even when there appears to be no such scriptural supplement, there may be an unwritten, though thoroughly well understood, convention among Christians of different denominations which decrees that some parts of the Bible are more important than others, and that while some types of behaviour and some attitudes are acceptable within the community of the faithful, others are not. In most cases, Christian denominationalism has developed as first one element, and then another, has been elevated to a position of pre-eminence in the life of a socially, culturally or tribally separate community. And as long as the community in question considers its separate existence worth preserving, these elements continue to be stressed. They may be doctrinally of the utmost importance; they may appear to the outsider to be of a devastating triviality: but when they serve to give a community of believers its own self-identity, they are never insignificant.

We may perhaps also note that the role of 'charismatic' leadership in the world of religion has often had a similar effect – that of dividing up a broader company of believers into small groups, depending each on the personality of a leader-interpreter. We have already discussed the phenomenon, and do not need to repeat what has already been said. But let us at least note that although one may conceivably serve two masters after a fashion, it is at least unnatural to have two fathers simultaneously. Bound by the deepest of emotional ties to their spiritual father, disciples inevitably affirm what he affirms, and reject what he rejects. The consequences for religious sectarianism are there for all to see, especially in those cases where the spiritual father-figure rests his case on his own supremely authoritative insights rather than on the cumulative tradition of which he is a living continuation. Moses David, the leader of the Children of God, though he interprets the New Testament, stands in no particular tradition: Swami Prabhupada, founder of the Hare Krishna movement in the west, carried further a centuries-old Hindu interpretative school. In both cases, they were and are supremely authoritative to their followers.

In following this line of argument, we have moved farther and farther into the area of small-scale religious movements. But are they 'religions' in the way in which we assume Christianity and Hinduism to be religions? Quantitatively, they are clearly not, since each exists only within a limited field of religious possibilities. But in the sense that 'sects' (of whatever origin) exist primarily as communities affirming each its own scale of values relative to things sacred and secular, they are, phenomenologically speaking, religions. Within each there will be seen the existential, intellectual, social and ethical concerns which we may identify as the marks of religion, and each will provide its adherents with a set of priorities, and a map of the universe.

In principle, therefore, as long as we understand by 'religions' identifiable organisations of believers, it may not seem to matter very much under which headings they have been traditionally sorted. They may be close together, or remote from one another. Provided that each separately is examined with a view to its history, structure, and self-understanding, as well as to the face it presents to the outside world, parallel or comparative study is never likely to be a waste of time.

*

But when we look at the actual practice of the study of religion in western universities, colleges and schools, we seldom or never find this principle operating. There (and leaving aside the study of the Ancient Near East and the Mediterranean world, which served as a necessary backdrop to the study of the Old and New Testaments, and was therefore entirely acceptable to theologians) it has been almost inevitably the case that the student in search of a living alternative to the Judaeo-Christian tradition has been pointed first of all in the direction of India. The reasons for this are intriguing but intricate. They are not unconnected with the position of India in the political, commercial and intellectual life of western countries, notably Britain. Throughout the whole of the nineteenth century, it was India which served as Europe's intellectual and spiritual idealised *alter ego*, and as a mirror in which generations of Europeans sought to see their spiritual selves as they might be. Above all, India seemed to many at that time to be strong in precisely those areas in which Europe was weak – in spirituality and depth of religious insight. Whether it was Swami Vivekananda who first generalised that 'the East' is spiritual while 'the West' is incurably materialist is something of an open question; but whoever first made the statement, it seemed to be true in 1900, and to the spiritually-minded it has seemed true ever since. And who could seriously deny the claim of India to represent the essence of 'eastern spirituality' and 'mysticism'? In comparison with India, China and Japan were far too remote and sheltered by linguistic and cultural barriers. The languages of India, on the other hand, were related to Latin and Greek, and could be learned, given a little time and trouble.

Generations of western travellers, administrators, soldiers, traders and missionaries knew India well (at least on the surface), and wrote libraries on their experiences.

All in all, then, the image of India was ever-present to the mind of the west during the heyday of 'comparative religion', between the 1850s and the 1950s. It is not surprising that its religions should have attracted so much attention, or that the student of religion should have felt its major group of traditions ('Hinduism') to be deserving of very special study. Whether most students ever actually came within hailing distance of the actualities of the religious life of India must on the other hand remain something of an open question.

The study of Hinduism as a first step in the multi-cultural study of religion was never without its risks. Today these are more marked than ever before. True, more students have actually visited India than would have been the case a few decades ago. But fewer have actually studied Indian languages (or other necessary aspects of Indian culture), and most have come to India rather as tourists than as travellers. Although some sections of Indian society have at one level accommodated to western customs and forms of cultural expression, there remain many more areas where this has scarcely even begun to happen, and these are practically inaccessible to the average western student. And partly due to the successes of Hindu-type new religious movements in the west (which in many cases represent not traditional Hindu values, but a small selection of Hindu notions carefully packaged and marketed to suit the western consumer), many visitors come carrying preconceived opinions about India and things Indian no less distorted than those which were current in the heyday of the Raj. As a rule, there is less chance of their being corrected by experience. If the textbook situation were better, then there might be less reason to worry; but the massively detailed tomes produced by yesterday's Indologists are in most cases both out of date and inaccessible outside the large libraries, and they are often not being replaced. It is in these days hard for the teacher to recommend a single up-to-date and reasonably comprehensive volume on the religions of India as they are actually practised; while in the matter of texts, although there are translations aplenty, too many are of dubious quality, and very few explain what today's western student most needs to have explained. In the case of Hindu India's most popular scripture the *Bhagavad Gita*, for instance, though there are literally dozens of translations into European languages, the ideal student's commentary has still not seen the light of day.

Far be it from me to discourage any student from attempting to study the religions of India. If carried out carefully, in full and conscious knowledge of the very great difficulties it involves, it is bound to be a worthwhile and satisfying exercise. But it does not provide the only – or even the best – alternative to the Judaeo-Christian tradition for the purposes of comparative study.

I have often wondered why, particularly in European universities and colleges, there should not have been more attention paid to Europe's pre-Christian beliefs and practices in the context of the study of religion. Although it might of course be argued that these – and here I am thinking in particular of the Celtic and Germanic religions – are no longer 'living' traditions in the sense that Hinduism and Buddhism are living and developing, they have made an important and lasting contribution to the life and thought of the whole of the western world. Why then should it be assumed that they can be studied only by linguists on the one hand, and by folklorists on the other? The west's great religious festivals are by no means wholly Christian: the word 'Easter', if we are to believe Bede, was the name of an Anglo-Saxon goddess of fertility (Eostre), while a very substantial part of our Christmas celebration is a direct continuation of the pre-Christian Germanic midwinter festival. Four of the names of the days of the week in English contain the names of Germanic gods; the British (and hence the American and Australian) countryside is full of Germanic place-names. The English language (and particularly the northern dialects) contains strings of Germanic and Scandinavian-derived words. But most important, perhaps, the religious *attitudes* of Europe retain far more of the Germanic and Celtic ethos than most people realise.

Now the point is this: allowing that the student of religion will want at some point to place religions side by side for the purpose of comparison, and recognising that close-at-hand traditions may partly meet this need, is it absolutely necessary for the rest to compare at a vast geographical and cultural distance, such as that which separates Europe and India? Might not an equally useful purpose be served by concentrating on successtive, but contrasting, phases of development in the *same* geographical area? And might not this alternative approach to 'the one and the many' avoid at least some of the more obvious risks connected with a careless and superficial interculturalism?

These risks are, I believe, fairly obvious – undue and conventional selectivity, which chooses not what is most important in an exotic tradition, but what it most accessible and superficially attractive; the tendency to rush into the juxtaposition of subjective images, rather than spend time working slowly with intractable and difficult material; and the tendency on the western student's part to treat the 'other' tradition as a mirror for his own concerns.

As against this, for the western student of religion to study the Celtic and Germanic past, though it is antiquarian in one sense, is in another a means of grasping something of his own cultural heritage. It also provides a paradigm of what happens when religions and cultures meet. It demonstrates something of the tenacity of popular beliefs and practices in pre-industrial society. It is also (and this I can attest from personal experience) a subject which very many students – perhaps because they are less alienated from the roots of their own culture than they suppose – find fascinating in its own right. Those who doubt this may perhaps reflect on the vast success of the writings of the late J.R.R. Tolkien.

*

Another type of comparative study which emerges naturally from these beginnings is *the regional project.* This may be either 'phenomenological' or historical.

It is quite startling how little attention is paid by many of today's students of religion to the cataloguing and interpreting of the religious beliefs and practices of their own world. The result is not only that the students themselves remain in most cases utterly ignorant of what is going on around them; but also that a vast amount of interesting and illuminating material remains ungathered and unanalysed. It is a number of years now since Geoffrey Parrinder, then a Methodist missionary, produced his book *Religion in an African City* (1951), with its fascinating account of the various levels of religious life in the Nigerian city of Ibadan. I am not suggesting that it would be at all feasible to carry out such a project in a megalopolis like London, Chicago or Sydney: but it can be done and should be done in smaller towns (say, less than 100,000 inhabitants). It would involve the techniques of the historian, the sociologist and the anthropologist, a good deal of participant observation and the gathering of much diverse material. But it has seldom or never been attempted at all thoroughly, and one cannot help wondering why.

Historical regional projects have of course been carried out from time to time, but I shall illustrate what I mean from one which has not. No one has ever written a consecutive account of the religious history of my own native region of North Lancashire and Cumbria. The area involved is less than a hundred miles from north to south, and only about fifty from east to west; and yet within these boundaries there is to be found a record in microcosm of practically the entire religious history of Britain. The megalith builders placed their stone circles on the Lake District hills (Castlerigg); the Celtic element is obscure, despite later references to Druids, but the Romans, among much else, left their altars to composite Romano-British deities, worshipped Mithras on the northern frontier (Carrawburgh), and perhaps Jesus Christ too (Lancaster). Celtic Christianity came there under the name of St. Patrick (Heysham). Scandinavian worshippers of Thor and Odin left their lasting mark, their 'hog-back' gravestones, their runic inscriptions and, once Christianised, their symbols on cross-shafts (Halton, Gosforth). In the middle ages, great monasteries were built (Furness Abbey, Cocker Sands), and as time went on, every development in the history of the Christian Church was reflected in some way or other in the area – including every variety of churchmanship, though especially Quakerism (George Fox languished in Lancaster Castle and lived at Swarthmore Hall), and the Keswick Holiness movement. And in the fullness of time, a small community of Gujerati Sufi Muslims settled in Lancaster.

It may be that there are not many parts of the world which have such a wealth of (in this case, uninvestigated) material in the history of religion. But it would surely not be difficult to devise similar programmes of regional study of religious life in many other parts of the world – programmes which would satisfy all the demands of comparative study and at the same time avoid the wild and subjective comparison of elements having no ascertainable connection with one another.

As far as the comparative exercise is concerned, we may perhaps sum up by saying that all knowledge involves an element of comparison across some frontier. The intellectual fashion of the past which involved the assumption that the comparison of 'religions' meant the evaluation of vast and complex '-isms' in relation to one another was always a mistake, and it is high time to discard whatever remains of its lingering influence. But religious traditions and communities can and should be placed side by side, even when they belong within ostensibly the same 'great tradition': the more they in fact have in common, the better we are able to recognise and evaluate that in which they differ. Sheer size is however no criterion at all. Such studies may be *synchronic*, in the sense that the phenomena they investigate exist at more or less the same time and have been produced in response to similar external pressures; or they may be *diachronic*, following a chronological sequence in a given area. Most fruitful of all, perhaps, is the study of an actual encounter between believers belonging to different traditions, in a definite place and at a given time, for then the issues involved stand out in peculiar clarity: I may perhaps be forgiven for citing my own study of the encounter of Hinduism and Christianity in India in the years before 1914 as an example (Sharpe, 1965). It is in such concrete situations that to speak of 'the comparative study of religion' still makes a great deal of sense.

How many 'religions' is it then necessary to study in order to understand 'religion'? It really does not matter. Perhaps there are no 'religions' – only those who believe, and because they believe, behave in a certain way. And in a sense, every specimen of *homo religiosus*, however we may want to label him (or her) is different from every other. Even if we do choose to call each separate organisation a 'religion', in one sense we shall find just as much inside one of them – if we know what we are looking for – as we shall find in half a dozen. If, on the other hand, all religion is one, then sheer old-fashioned curiosity may drive us to the ends of the earth to find evidence of its workings. There can be no hard-and-fast rules (and many of what we have been tempted to think of as rules have been no more than intellectual fashions). Least of all do we need to feel impelled to go to the remote, the exotic and the inaccessible for our material. It is all around us, if (as I say) we only know where and how to look.

Seven

Four 'Modes' of Religion

We have seen that in principle, practically any religious tradition contains within itself sufficient variety to occupy a normal student during a normal lifetime, but that parallel studies between one tradition and another are both useful and necessary, even when those traditions may sort under the same textbook heading. But religion is not one simple thing, nor does it fulfil one single function. As well as the customary geographical and historical divisions between one 'religion' and another, it is therefore advisable to keep in mind the possibility – indeed the certainty – that wherever we look in the world of religion, different needs are being met and different functions fulfilled.

It is not always easy to convince people that religion is, in fact, multi-functional. All too often the talk among intellectuals has been of 'the essence of religion' – a single powerfully compelling idea which is taken to be absolute and final, a sentiment, a notion, an attitude which is self-authenticating and without which religion cannot exist. Philosophically or theologically speaking, the discussion about 'Essences' is not without its point. Functionally speaking, however, the discussion has to be carried on in different terms. It is less a matter of what function or functions religion might, or *ought to*, fulfil when it is at its best, than of the possible range of functions which it *actually* fulfils under varying circumstances.

To the functional question, many of the existing textbooks have very little to contribute. Commonly they divide up their material tribe by tribe, country by country, culture by culture, and follow each separate path as it winds its way through its own history. In terms of straightforward chronicle, this is reasonable enough. Without the kind of elementary historical knowledge which this kind of study provides, whatever else there may be to the study of religion is bound to be at best elusive, and may at worst be totally inaccessible. There is an elementary craft involved in the study of religion, which is as indispensable as the practising of scales is to the budding musician, and it is hard to imagine how else this craft can be learned than by the assimilation of a certain amount of factual historical information. But the acquisition of such information can never be an end in itself, since even when a great deal of it has been absorbed, the student may still be at a loss to know what to make of the *totality* of the phenomenon 'religion'.

Nor is the problem necessarily solved through the division-of-labour approach which shares the field of religion out among technical subject specialists – philosophers, psychologists, historians, sociologists and the rest. The division is certainly convenient, and many functional questions can be dealt with by this means. Where a company of specialists in one or another of these areas meets together and talks together in a language which all can understand, much may be achieved, and inter-disciplinary projects are becoming more and more common. But whatever the more flexible and sensitive scholars may from time to time say, the main drawback here is simply the intrusive 'human factor', and the tendency of some scholars to want to defend their own territories, perhaps even by refusing the very cooperation which would place their individual efforts in perspective.

But there is another drawback here. This division of the field of religion has been made less on a basis of the nature of the material to be dealt with than by the accidental criteria of the recent history of western scholarship. Philologists who study religion, for instance, can only study its verbal expressions: when they pass beyond the texts, they cease to be philologists, and run professional risks. Psychologists of religion tend to want to hold up their heads in psychological, and not only religious, company, and set their sights accordingly. And academic reputation being a fragile thing at the best of times (particularly to scholars without tenure), a necessary and fruitful specialisation can all too easily become a nervous clinging to a set of 'respectable' techniques and a failure to appreciate (sometimes even to understand) the techniques of others.

I am not saying that technical specialisation of this kind has no role to play in the study of religion. Clearly it has. But if religion as a subject for study can be tackled only on the basis of arbitrary or conventional divisions of the kind I have been describing, what hope is there of anyone ever arriving at an 'integral understanding' of religion, given the vast range of its manifestations, its long history, and the need for so much specialist knowledge in dealing with its separate parts? Is it not true to say that none of us, strictly speaking, can ever know enough or stand far enough away to view the totality? And this being so, is it not better to leave such matters to the seers (or to the dilettantes), meanwhile cultivating our own little gardens?

Certainly, if the operative criteria are all quantitative, then we must all, sooner or later, retreat in shame and confusion, since we can never know enough of this side of human history. If they are academically professional, then few of us have the opportunity, let alone the specialist training, to master more than one or two techniques. But what if there are other criteria, which are functional rather than quantitative or narrowly professional, which divide the field without distorting or destroying it, and which are applicable to religion both in its local and its more general manifestations? I believe that there are such criteria, and the remainder of this chapter will be devoted to an attempt to explain them.

*

Religion, whatever its ultimate origins in this world or outside it, involves human beings in a variety of attitudes and types of behaviour. We may be more or less elaborate in deciding how many of these there may be, but *as an irreducible minimum* I shall propose four, which I shall call (not being able to think of a better word) functional *modes* of religious belief and behaviour.

I do not wish to claim any particular originality for my fourfold division of the field. Many similar attempts have been made in the past, and I had been using my classification for some time before I found that the Swedish scholar Helmer Ringgren has a practically identical four-part scheme in his book *Religionens form och funktion* (1968). Other scholars have produced more elaborate patterns, and I should like to quote one such example.

In his book *Secular Education and the Logic of Religion* (1968) and elsewhere, Ninian Smart has put forward a theory of a six-dimensional structure of religion. His six 'dimensions' are divided up into two groups of three. The first he labels as *parahistorical*, that is, going beyond the bounds of history as normally understood; the second comprises that which has to do with the *historical* phenomena of religion as these appear in the world. Smart's total scheme looks like this:

The parahistorical	1. Doctrinal dimension 2. Mythological dimension 3. Ethical dimension
The historical	4. Ritual dimension 5. Experiential dimension 6. Social dimension

This scheme, perhaps because at the time when it was put forward it represented a new and creative way of looking at the totality of religious belief and practice, has won considerable support and is often quoted. But I have never been altogether happy with it, for two reasons.

The first is the way in which it is set out, which leads one to suppose that the lower the number, the more important the element in question: the parahistorical appears to be more important than the historical, doctrine more important than myth and ethics, and so on. Perhaps in Smart's view there is a scale of values involved, and certainly most students have distinct preferences. But in most cases these days it would probably be argued that 'Dimension 5' is the most important of all, and 'Dimension 1' perhaps the least important. This impression may be wrong, and in any case popular preferences ought not to force the student into dangerous value-judgments. But if a scheme like this is to be adopted, it perhaps ought to be set out differently.

But more seriously, I wonder whether all of these 'dimensions' in fact fall into the same type of category. Two of them at least, the 'mythological' and 'ritual' dimensions, appear to me to be more matters of *content* than do the other four. If myth and ritual are to be accepted as 'dimensions' of religion (and far be it from me to deny that they are genuinely part of a religious totality), then there are other, similar 'dimensions' which demand to be taken into consideration as well. It could be said, for instance, that there is a legal dimension, a musical dimension, a symbolical dimension, a spatial dimension, and many more such dimensions. But it would be hard to maintain that there is a musical or a legal *mode*, which is an intrinsic part of the structure of religion, without which it cannot be understood. Myth and ritual can be taken out of religion altogether, and though religion may suffer in the process, its basic fourfold structure will not be threatened. Myth and ritual I in fact believe to be phenomena, observables, and therefore part of that which we are trying to analyse rather than categories or functions. ('Dimension' in Smart's scheme does not easily translate into 'function'.)

My four-fold scheme I should therefore like to present as follows: religion operates, humanly speaking, in four functional modes. Opinions may differ as to what to call them, but we may perhaps use the labels:

1. Existential
2. Intellectual
3. Institutional
4. Ethical

Each has an appropriate noun, characterising its dominant content. Again we may choose from among the available options:

1. *Faith* in the sense of *fiducia*, 'trust'
2. *Beliefs* in the sense of those statements which one gives conscious assent (*assensus*)
3. *Organisations* within which (1) and (2) are held and maintained, and by which they are transmitted
4. *Conduct* vis-à-vis the members of (3) and others.

I am not saying that from the point of view of the one who is attempting to understand religion, any one of these is intrinsically any more important than any of the others. However, individuals, whether believers or students, have their own characteristic emphases.

Taking believers first, in the life of the individual or the community, one mode is very often regarded as being more important, 'central', 'essential' than the others (either by deliberate choice or by inherited tradition). In such cases, one of the following patterns is likely to emerge: (see diagram on p. 96).

This diagram may not be entirely self-explanatory, but what it is intended to show is the way in which, in the life of the individual believer (or the community of which he is part) one or other 'mode' of religion serves as a gateway to all the others. Shortly I shall proceed to a brief discussion of the various ways in which this principle operates. For the moment let me merely say that, in terms

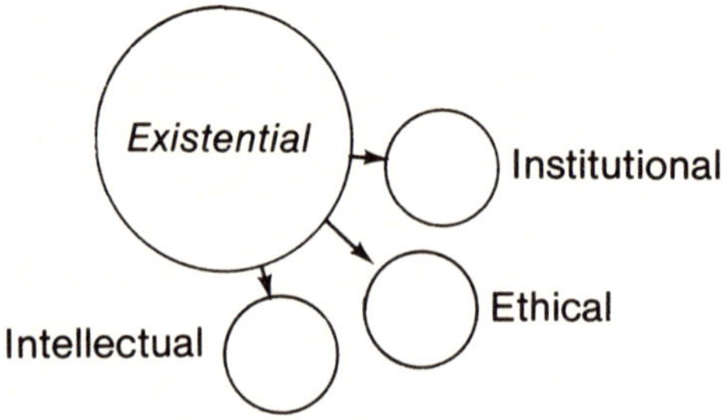
Existential
Institutional
Ethical
Intellectual

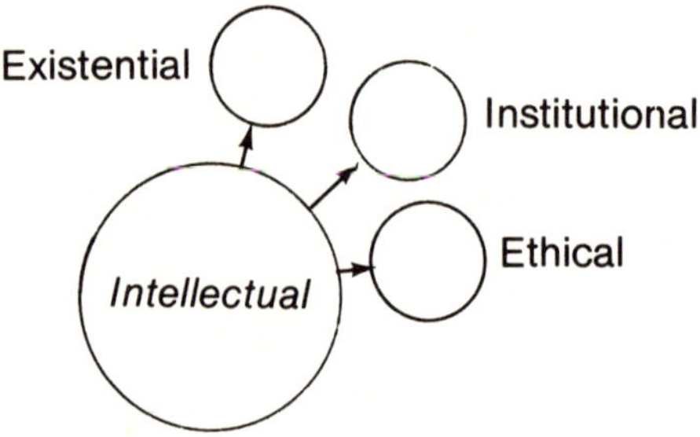
Existential
Institutional
Ethical
Intellectual

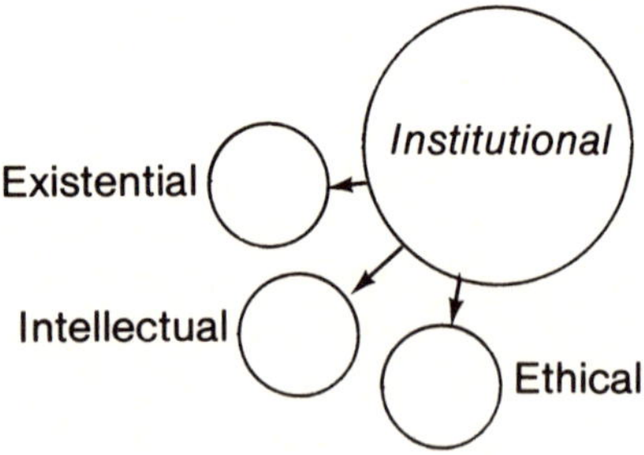
Institutional
Existential
Intellectual
Ethical

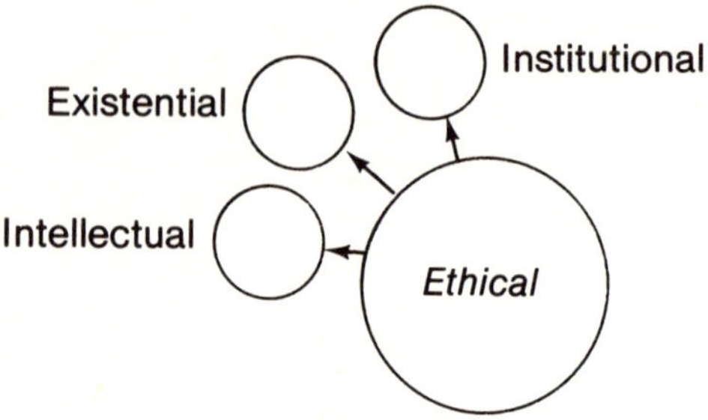
Institutional
Existential
Intellectual
Ethical

of the supernatural or the transcendent, in each case it is through the dominant element that (to use a Swedenborgian term) the 'influx' of the unseen world comes. Each, in other words, supplies the symbols by means of which that world is described and evaluated.

Since this pattern extends to ideologies and to human value-systems generally, it is equally one which the student ought also to be able to recognise as operative within other segments of the society of which he or she is part. Politics, too, might be analysed in a similar fourfold fashion, as might those various pressure-groups to which most have belonged at one time or another. What this means in practice is that there are very few students (or others) who do not have a built-in preference for one 'mode' of religious life over against the others – even though, as far as they are concerned, the preference may have originated from other sources entirely. But this preference will very often then carry over into the study of religion – not always with the best or most desirable results.

Now, however, we must consider in general terms the characteristics of each 'mode' separately.

The existential mode: the circle of faith

This is the purely individual aspect of religion: the dominant factor here is the unquestioning acceptance of the reality of the supernatural/transcendent order (under whatever set of images), and a sense of dependence upon and trust in the influence of that order. It involves the emotions and the will, 'faith', 'trust', 'love', 'fear', 'devotion', 'confidence', 'security'. At one pole it may be a simple fear in face of the workings of an incomprehensible 'power'. At the opposite pole it gives rise to the mystic's sense of oneness with the Real. In between, there are all the varieties of individual 'religious experience'.

It is hardly necessary to stress what a great value is placed on 'religious experience' in our day, at least by those who verbalise their religion. Perhaps the tendency is strongest in Protestant Christianity, where it is not uncommon to find such expressions as 'conversion experience', 'born-again experience' and even (somewhat oddly) 'worship experience' being used. There are fairly obvious reasons why this should be so – among them the individualism of the later Protestant tradition and the indirect impact of the psychology of religion in investigating the inner workings of what was once called 'the religious consciousness'. But that is incidental to the point at issue.

The point is that there is in religion a deep, and perhaps in the last resort inexplicable, conviction on the individual's part of the existence and reality of a non-natural, non-sensory order of being; and an equally deep conviction that it affects his life, and that he can make contact with it. What 'it' may be called, and how 'it' may be described, are on the other hand infinitely variable. Usually the images resorted to are not plucked out of the air, but are related to whatever the individual may have been taught to expect with regard to the unseen world – and here the individual aspect of religion passes over into the corporate area of tradition. What is experienced may be well defined – for instance in conforming to well-known icons or quoting an already known sacred scripture; or it may be totally amorphous, and communicate nothing save an inexplicable sense of 'wholeness' and well-being. But whatever the details, the experience itself is, so far as the subject is concerned, entirely self-authenticating. It does not permit of analysis or even discussion, though it may be compared with similar experiences which others have had.

Clearly, however, not all those who belong within the general orbit of religion *have* had self-authenticating personal experiences of this kind. It is not uncommon, therefore, to find within religious traditions many who simply refer, in the matter of experience, to the experiences of others – kings, priests, prophets, gurus, 'charismatic' leaders, even (oddly enough) academics. But of course the act of submission, allegiance and acceptance which this involves is also an experience, though it might be argued that it sorts rather under the social mode of religion than under the existential. Nor would most want to claim that 'collective experience' or 'the experience of belonging' is very likely to lead in the direction of mysticism.

A very brief word about 'mysticism' may not be out of place at this stage.

The term 'mysticism' itself permits of no precise definition, and its use in almost any discussion leads to untold confusion – so much so, that I have sometimes felt that it ought to be, if not strictly excluded from scholarly discussion, at least used very sparingly and with the greatest of care. All that one can say is that in so far as it may be taken to refer to anything definite within the phenomenology (rather than the psychology) of religion, it is to the area of 'religious experience' – to a subjective sense of oneness with the ground of all being, to visions, voices, and 'altered states of consciousness' in which the human senses cease to function normally. Mysticism, we may say, is related to individual, subjective religious experience quantitatively, rather than qualitatively. If we may accept that, in Evelyn Underhill's words, mysticism is '... the expression of the innate tendency of the human spirit towards complete harmony with the transcendental order', and is to be shunned as an excuse for 'dilute transcendentalism, vapid symbolism' and other spiritual disorders (Underhill, 1930: xiv), then on the one hand it is not something unnatural, being 'innate'; while on the other, since it strives for 'complete' harmony with the transcendental order, doubtless there are many intermediate stages, in which a measure of harmony, or temporary harmony is felt to have been reached.

As between 'religious experience' and 'mysticism', the student is faced with precisely the same problem, however: that of knowing how to evaluate the first-hand testimony which is the only possible source of information. To the statements 'Last night I saw a vision', 'I have heard the voice of God', 'I know that my sins have been forgiven', no response is possible, save respectful attention. Since these statements can be neither proved nor disproved by reference to any external authority, it is totally impossible to brand them 'true' or 'false', though perhaps some reference may be made to the consequences, if any, to which they lead. What must not be done, on the other hand, is to regard statements of this kind as of no consequence in the study of religion. Without such experiences – perhaps more especially experiences involving 'altered states of consciousness' – it is very probable that there would be no religion to study. Again it must be stressed that this does not mean that every 'believer' has actually had such experiences. But they clearly provide an initial impulse without which religion could scarcely have begun; and in their total absence, religion in the end becomes transmuted into something else – an ideology, a club, a pressure group – since its members are able to relate only to one another, and not to any supernatural or transcendent order whatsoever.

Probably, therefore, the experiential mode of religion will always tend to be regarded (in theory at least) as of more importance than other modes – by those who have had what they believe to be direct experience of the supernatural/transcendent, since it injects the certainty of personal conviction into the world of customs, rules and theories; and by those who have not, since in many cases they may wish that they had (even, let it be said, to the extent of pretending to have had experiences when they have not).

Even the religiously indifferent, or the outright enemies of religion, tend to share this view in a slightly topsy-turvy way, it being part of socialist ideology that religion can be tolerated only to the extent that it remains discreetly hidden and keeps itself out of the public arena. The believer is entirely free to believe, and to have whatever experiences he chooses, provided that his beliefs do not spill over into the area of 'real' power – public life, politics and economics.

But this is not to say, either on the positive or the negative side, that 'experience' is the whole of religion, or even that it is the 'essence' of religion. Those who claim that 'experience will decide' in this matter have already defined religion in terms of their own personal experiences, or what they take the experiences of others to be. Often, therefore, there is a tendency to undervalue and distort whatever else there may be to the totality of religious life. Intellectual beliefs – doctrines, dogmas, creeds, theological statements – are classified as unnecessary accretions, which serve to obscure rather than to illuminate the Real. Organisational forms are criticised on similar grounds, while even the ethical may in extreme cases be either ignored or left to the individual's personal insight to settle (the position of 'situation ethics').

The intellectual mode: the circle of beliefs

The dominant factor in the second functional 'mode' of religion is the formulation of statements *about* the supernatural or the transcendent order. To these statements, individuals and groups give their intellectual or formal assent (or not, as the case may be). Those who do so, thereby qualify themselves as members of the community ('of the faith'); those who do not, are heretics, foreigners, barbarians, 'lesser breeds without the law'. It is here that there are formed doctrines, dogmas, theologies and philosophies – attempts to say something precise about God, the gods or Ultimate Reality, deduced from individual and collective experiences of the kind we have been discussing, interpreted as acts of revelation.

It is useful to distinguish between the kind of attitude which is held to these statements and that which is held to the Ultimate

Reality itself. The latter is best called 'faith' (*fiducia*, trust); the former 'belief' (*assensus*, intellectual or conventional acceptance and acquiescence). Not that the two are always distinguished in practice. Very often they are not, or they appear not to be. Christian creeds in English have oscillated between 'I believe' and 'we believe', though the Latin form of the Nicene Creed begins *Credo* [I believe] *in unum Deum* ... The intention is here both formal and personal. Alternatively, one might draw a distinction between the prepositions used: the 'existential mode' involves faith, trust, or belief *in* a revelation or hierophany, a manifestation of the sacred; the 'intellectual mode' has to do with faith, trust or belief *that* a statement *about* the hierophany is a trustworthy statement. It is proper to refer to these acceptable statements in the plural, as 'beliefs'. Faith and trust, on the other hand, hardly allow themselves to be cast in plural form.

Formulated beliefs arise just as soon as it becomes desirable or necessary to communicate the content of a tradition to coming generations, or to outsiders. They also arise where it is necessary to state what a tradition does *not* contain – which is one of the reasons why the early history of any tradition is apt to contain a good deal of controversy over doctrinal points.

The anti-intellectualism which condemns theologies and philosophies as attempts made by cunning and unscrupulous priests to pull the wool over the eyes of (or blow holy smoke in the eyes of) ordinary believers is well enough known. ('When priests quarrel among themselves, that's theology, and that's something ordinary folk don't need to worry their heads about.') It does not need to be taken too seriously, however, as an argument. Not that it has never happened. But it has happened far less often than the opponents of religion suppose. Any attempt, as we have said, to communicate any religious impulse to the young, to students, to outsiders by way of mission, leads very soon to intellectual formulations – and artistic and dramatic representations – of its meaning and implications. An attempt has to be made to systematise teachings, to explain the role of the founder-prophet, to describe rituals and the correct way to carry them out, and to draw out the implications of all this for life in the community and the everyday world. That this leads in the course of time to a somewhat specialised vocabulary is neither reprehensible nor even remarkable. For one thing, it is not intended to replace, but merely to draw out the consequences of, faith and devotion. Although in some cases there may be a certain element of secrecy involved, in that the deepest levels of the faith may be hidden from the uninitiated, total secrecy in these matters is in fact very uncommon. And thirdly, the intellectual constructions of every religious tradition are based on cause-and-effect categories: if A and B are 'true' (within the circle of trust in a revelation having taken place), then the logical consequences are C and D.

Admittedly, though, there are many believers whose minds work most easily on this level, and who regard the 'objective' deliverances of an intellectual orthodoxy as preferable to (and above all safer than) unbridled 'subjectivism' in religious matters. The subjective is all too liable to be non-rational, if not irrational, and is feared accordingly by the rational mind. Within the circle of beliefs there are both those who adhere firmly to what their tradition prescribes, and those who to some extent go their own individual way, pursuing their own intellectual quests at a level of theoretical abstraction. In the former case, the community and its rituals and conventions may be all-important; in the latter, the community may be of value chiefly as a phenomenon to react against. In the former case, there will be a strong emphasis on the faithful performance of duty; in the latter, the individual's chief duty is the duty to think.

The institutional mode: the circle of organisations

Within the orbit of religion, there are natural organisations and voluntary organisations. The former begin with families and extend to tribes, castes and nations: those into which the individual is born or incorporated legally (by marriage or naturalisation). The latter are assemblies of individuals and families who have at some stage chosen to join them – though these very soon begin to grow naturally, as children are born and incorporated into the community. Natural, or ethnic, organisations are normally closed to outsiders. At the 'primal' level, one cannot join a tribe to which one does not belong (save, perhaps, by marriage). In Hindu terms, one cannot join a caste. But the greater part of religious organisations of the present day both permit and encourage outsiders to join, under certain conditions. Usually this is a matter of personal conviction leading to conversion and initiation. In today's partly secularised western society, the 'voluntary principle' has been so long established that it is virtually impossible to argue for any other:

either one belongs to a community of 'believers' whose principles one has accepted fully consciously, or one does not. All else, it is supposed, is mechanical and second-best.

Here we may merely note that, in world terms, the voluntary principle is both recent and local. To be sure, there have been times in practically every part of the world where a new religious tradition has made its appearance and individual or (more usually) mass conversions have taken place. The spread of Buddhism, Christianity and Islam have all followed this pattern. Most past conversions took place as a consequence, not of a vast number of individual decisions, but of a ruler's decision on behalf of his (or her) people. The head of the 'sacred community', in other words, chose to give allegiance to a new god or a new teacher. On the lower level, families and tribes were hardly disturbed. Sacred rituals continued to be observed (not least those involving reverence paid to ancestors); sacred sites remained sacred; seasonal festivals were still celebrated. In many cases, individuals were simply not in a position to make a decision on their own behalf, without reference to the remainder of the social organisation to which they 'naturally' belonged. This was the pattern of early mediaeval Europe, as Germanic paganism gave way to Christianity, and it has applied to many 'mass movements' – to Buddhism, Christianity, Islam – in many parts of the world since then.

But in post-Reformation European Christianity, and throughout the whole of American history, only the individualistic, voluntary principle has obtained. To be sure, in time even 'voluntary' organisations develop something of a 'tribal' character; but movement from one to another is fairly common nevertheless.

It is an aspect of religious life to which students have in the past given far too little attention, that voluntary religious organisations offer human fellowship before they offer anything else. They may well function as a 'substitute family', under the guidance of a 'father' or 'mother', offering a mixture of authority, guidance, discipline and human warmth to individuals who feel alienated from other (often 'natural') communities. This pattern – which is most powerful in the case of today's 'new religious movements' – may mean that the individual is attracted for reasons having little or nothing to do with what the group actually believes or claims to believe. Only gradually will he discover the faith and beliefs of the community, and very often these will ultimately be accepted as a mark of self-identification with its values, along with such outward symbols as dress, taboos, language and scales of values.

Those for whom the organisational mode of religion is the most important (and one suspects that in fact these are legion), are often content with the words 'we believe ...' Direct personal inquiry into the foundations of faith and beliefs is uncommon, partly because it may appear to threaten the solidarity of the group on the one hand, and the individual's place in the group on the other. 'Heresy' (wrong beliefs) and 'syncretism' (mixed beliefs) are both dangers to be avoided, for the same reasons. Ethical conduct will again very often follow the lines which the group accepts as a mark of identification, and there is a very real fear of stepping out of line.

All these characteristics are to be seen very clearly in the case of migrant communities, who retain their identity in a new and sometimes perplexing environment partly by means of the collective values which membership in a church, synagogue, mosque or temple provides. Otherwise they are as dominant in everyday western religiosity as they are in the 'primal' or 'tribal' context. But they are little understood and even less appreciated by the intense and the intellectual.

The ethical mode: the circle of duties

For something like two centuries now, western religion has been overwhelmingly concerned with matters of ethical conduct, sometimes to the virtual exclusion of all else. Not that the ethical was previously unimportant: on the contrary, the gods have always made demands of men and women in respect of the way they must behave toward one another. But the process of secularisation (to be discussed more fully in our next chapter) has led to this result among many, that even when the gods have been expelled from their sanctuaries, the laws which they once were believed to have laid down continue in force.

In 'primal' and 'archaic' societies, law is almost inevitably inseparable from religion (prompting some scholars to wonder whether religion might not have begun chiefly as a matter of 'supernatural sanctions' lending authority to precept). To the question, 'Why act in a particular way?' the final answer will always be, 'Because God (or the gods) has decreed it'. The gods and their messengers are the law-givers, the priests their interpreters. But laws such as these commonly operate only within a well-defined community. On the inside, the strictest standards obtain: to those outside, one may behave without restraint (as the Dark Ages discovered in face of the Huns, Goths, Vandals and Vikings). We for our part speak of universals in the moral sphere – human rights, freedoms and justice – and whether or not we are prepared to consider the possibility of 'universal religion', often assume that there must be some form of global morality, to which all ought to conform.

In modern Western terms, therefore, where a narrowing of the frontiers of religion has taken place, it has very often involved the weakening of the first three functional modes of religion and a great emphasis on religion's ethical mode and function. Where the 'essence' of religion is discussed (and this applies to other religious traditions as well as to Christianity), the final result is often that this is taken to consist largely in an attitude of love, respect, compassion and helpfulness to human beings as such, virtually irrespective of the communities to which they may happen to belong. Other important consequences follow – for instance, that the religious believer is expected to be committed to non-violence, if not to absolute pacifism, and that the practicalities of religion are closely related to programmes of social action.

It is here that a serious difficulty arises for today's student, for the simple reason that in human history very few religious traditions have ever thought in these terms. As we have pointed out, in the vast majority of cases, strict ethical standards have been operative only *within* the community of believers. Over against 'the others', on the other hand, no ethical restraints need apply. 'Holy' or 'just' wars have been assumed to be inevitable and in some cases indeed desirable if individuals and groups can be identified as aggressors – and human nature being what it is, there are always aggressors to be found somewhere. At times, this age-old attitude has divided co-religionists (between 1914 and 1918, all the major belligerents save Turkey were outwardly 'Christian' countries, praying for victory apparently to the same God), which fact may incidentally serve as a brake on the text-book assumption that, at the time, Christianity was *one* religion, in the terms discussed in our last chapter. But we cannot pursue this line of reasoning further on this occasion.

To the religionist whose chief categories are ethical, almost all the other functional modes of religion tend to be pushed to the periphery and not infrequently ignored altogether. Personal religious experience, particularly that involving 'altered states of consciousness', is disdained as a self-indulgent flight from 'reality'. Intellectual reflection is permissible only to the extent that it addresses itself to the ethical question: otherwise it is 'irrelevant'. The social forms of religion are wherever possible reshaped into pressure groups, and where this proves impossible they are condemned as 'ghettoes', 'God's frozen people', 'the comfortable pew' and the like, and abandoned for more responsive organisations. These are of course extreme conditions; but even in much less extreme cases, the individual and collective conscience is perhaps today's most powerful religious instrument. I am sure that there is no need to elaborate the point further. The evidence is there for all to see.

*

These, then, are the four major functions which religion has filled, and fills, in human experience. To avoid misunderstanding, it must be emphasised that none of the four commonly exists in total isolation from all the others, and that in most cases, a tradition (or a community, or an individual) will exhibit all four in varying degrees. To take two examples from present-day Christianity, on the Conservative Evangelical side the main emphasis tends to be placed on a combination of the first and the fourth – personal faith leading to ethical seriousness. On the liberal wing of Protestant opinion, on the other hand, the most important are probably the fourth and the second, in that order – ethical concern supported by intellectual arguments.

Among the rank and file of believers, however, there can be little doubt that it is 'the circle of organisations' and the experience of belonging to a familiar and concerned family of faith which is of the most importance.

For the student's part, since there will always be varying temperaments and personal preferences to be taken into account, it should finally be stressed that religion always involves all four, and that each needs to be given due attention when evaluating the whole. It goes without saying that this will not always be easy. A student strongly attracted in today's terms to an ethical interpretation of religion may find it hard to investigate the ecstasies of the mystics, the rituals of a mediaeval cathedral, and much else besides. But the attempt must be made if religion is to be grasped in its full range of expressions and functions.

Eight
The Process of Seularisation

It is only in the pages of textbooks that religions are static, fixed doctrinal and ritual systems which permit of no revision. This is not the place to reflect again on the intellectual fashions which once made western scholars suppose that each 'religion' could be encapsulated in a container of a particular shape and size. Doubtless one of the reasons had to do with the way in which yesterday's 'comparative religion' concentrated on the religions of the past, which at a certain point in time had stopped developing. But beyond this we may simply note that the tendency was to describe a religion in terms of its highest ideals, and to assume that these were substantially unchangeable. The consequences are there for everybody to see, in volume after volume of 'facts' about the world religions, their deities, doctrines, rituals and the like.

Living religions, however, are never static for very long at a time. On the contrary: they are always on the move, always under pressure from outward circumstances, always being challenged by alternative world-views, always rethinking their positions and creating new explanations of what they believe about the world and man's place in it. There will of course be times when a religious tradition may appear to be more or less static. A people who live in isolation, comparatively free from external pressures, may be able to live a religious life which runs smoothly along the deep grooves of tradition and custom. But let an intrusive element enter the social picture, by migration, conquest, trade, mission, revolution or whatever, and old certainties may collapse almost overnight.

Often in the past we have simply not known how the average believer has reacted to the kind of religious change which comes about as a result of these and similar pressures. We may surmise that in every case thee will have been a mixture of responses, ranging all the way from alarm to satisfaction, with many either remaining indifferent or prepared to play follow-my-leader into a world of new ideas and new possibilities. Today, however, the signs of religious change are all about us, and its processes and effects simply cannot be ignored by the student. It has to be investigated – though largely from the standpoint of the diagnostician: the prescribing of remedies must be left in other hands.

Yesterday's authorities were not always at their best when it came to reading the signs of the times, perhaps in some cases because they had a vision of the way in which they *wanted* religion to develop. On other occasions, developments took place which they had no way of anticipating. In 1932, the classical scholar Arthur Darby Nock, contemplating the massive solidity of the Roman Catholic Church, wrote:

> This majestic structure is likely to have a very long life as it stands; if I were to have a chance of seeing the world in 2432 ... I should confidently expect to find the Latin Mass being sung with the same gestures and dogmatic theology being taught according to the principles of St. Thomas Aquinas (Nock, 1972: I, 339).

Nock could not have been more mistaken. Yet had he reflected more deeply on social history and the history of ideas, he might have been more cautious. A couple of years earlier, Winston Churchill had recorded that in his generation, everything had changed:

> Scarcely anything material or established which I was brought up to believe was permanent and vital, has lasted. Everything I was sure or taught to be sure was impossible, has happened. (Churchill, 1959: 74 f.).

And looking back on the mathematical physics of the years just before the turn of the century, Alfred North Whitehead was to reflect in late life:

> By the turn of the century, nothing, absolutely nothing was left that had not been challenged, if not shaken; not a single major concept. (Whitehead, 1954: 215).

One would perhaps not anticipate the same wholesale renewal to take place in religion, partly because of religion's claim to concern itself with truth which lies beyond the reach of the world of phenomena. If the world is no more than a set of stage properties on which a cosmic drama is played out, then the changes of which Churchill and Whitehead speak may in the end by of very little significance. But to the student, religion is more than the sum total of its metaphysical teachings: it is equally its varied *modus operandi* in the world. And as far as this side of the business is concerned, the dominant present-day words, in religion as in all else, are renewal, expansion, decline, decay. Things are not made any easier when the same phenomenon can be greeted by one party as an advance and by another as a disaster – as in the case of the abandonment of the Latin Mass by the Roman Catholic Church.

The commonest blanket term used by scholars is, however, 'secularisation'. It describes a process of religious change in which ultimate authority passes from some 'religious' source – a scripture, a community, a hierarchy, a council – to a non-religious, or secular body – a parliament, a political party, a trades union, an amorphous company of scientists. But as is usual in religious affairs, the experts are agreed neither on what the phenomenon ought to be called, nor on the precise limits which need to be set to its working. Part of the problem here has had to do with the sheer volume of writing which has been produced on the subject in recent years. The process has of late been moving faster and faster, with the result that scholars have been falling over one another in the attempt to record its convolutions and to pin them down conceptually. An indirect consequence has been that sociologists of religion have more and more tended to discuss the phenomenon less in relation to what is actually happening than in relation to one another's theories about it. This is never very satisfying to the phenomenologist of religion, and in some cases can be very irritating indeed – though I do not propose to give examples.

In the world of religion there has always been something of a tension between 'conservative' and 'liberal' forces, between those for whom a sacred tradition is something to be preserved, taught and developed for the sake of the insights which it is believed to contain, and those for whom religion is always faced with new frontiers to be crossed. To the traditionalist, the frontier is always a dangerous boundary between the safe and the unsafe, cosmos and chaos; to the frontiersman, tradition is almost always a burden which prevents freedom of action. Neither fully appreciates the other's point of view, and both suspect the cautious souls who nail their colours to the fence and try to mediate between the positions. On the conservative side there is the priest, whose *raison d'être* rests in the way in which he (or she) preserves sacred tradition; on the liberal side there is the prophet, who is prepared to discard anything and everything for the sake of his calling to confront the world with the message: 'Thus says the Lord!' The priestly mind is seldom able to look on the secularisation process with equanimity, since it threatens so many of the values for which he stands. To the prophetic consciousness, on the other hand, secularisation may well appear in the light of a liberation from useless and outworn conventions.

Fortunately, perhaps, the phenomenologist of religion does not need to play the role of either priest or prophet, but rather the role of analyst and diagnostician. Convinced of the vast importance of the secularisation process, he is none the less also convinced that it is complex and many-sided, and that each time it occurs the evidence needs to be dealt with on its own merits.

In the mid-1960s, the 'prophetic' message of secularisation was being proclaimed by a number of Christian scholars, of whom Harvey Cox was one of the most widely read. In his book *The Secular City* (1965), he defined secularisation as '... the historical process, almost certainly irreversible, in which society and culture are delivered from tutelage to religious and closed metaphysical world-views' (Cox, 1965: 20). Elsewhere in the same book he distinguished between secularisation and 'secularism' in these words:

> Secularisation is a liberating process. It dislodges ancient oppressions and overturns stultifying conventions. It turns man's social and cultural life over to him, demanding a constant expenditure of vision and competence. Secularism short-circuits the secular revolution by freezing it into a new world-view. It clips the wings of emancipation and fixes society on the pin of another orthodoxy. (ibid.: 86).

In both these quotations, the operative word is *process*. Secularisation is not a thing; it is a chain of events, tending toward the replacement of one type of authority by another. It must always be distinguished from 'secularism', which in practice actually *is* the new authority – the absolute and unquestioned authority of the secular agency in matters involving the life of society.

However, before proceeding further, it should perhaps be noted that in present-day India, the word 'secularism' has taken on the rather special meaning of a social order in which no one religion is favoured over any other. It refers not to the absence of religion, but to the plurality of religions in a state which cannot afford to have favourites. Indian secularism does not aim to suppress or replace religion, but merely to keep religious considerations at a distance from the day-to-day workings of government.

Secularisation, then, is a process. It is generally assumed to be a world-wide process. The historian Herbert Butterfield wrote in 1960:

> Not merely in the West, but over the entire globe, there must come sooner or later a dissolution of the traditional hereditary systems of officially imposed or conventionally accepted religions. Our natural science, our technology, our rationalism and the superficial parts of our secular culture which are easily transmissible are already producing a remarkable transformation in other continents. They are bound to have the same dissolvent effects upon the traditional systems of India, Japan and China as they have upon the Christian tradition and heritage of European countries. (Butterfield, 1960:18).

Here and there, in face of this fact, attempts have been made to persuade the representatives of the religions of the world to band together to oppose its encroachment. Secularisation apparently leads to secularism, to unbelief, to godlessness; and if the world religions can agree on nothing else, they ought to be able to agree that this end result is a Bad Thing. Therefore let them join forces across the frontiers to fight against it. At a Christian missionary conference in 1928, a Quaker leader, Rufus M. Jones, stated:

> The civilisation which we have been building is inadequate for man's life and for his complete spiritual health. The world of business and industry and secular aims starves and dries up the soul, even where it does not corrupt and defile. It is not possible to live up to the full height of man's potential being without drawing upon the deeper resources of the spirit ... (Jones, 1928: 321).

Although Jones believed the antidote to be found in Christianity, he was nevertheless able to address himself also to 'the other religions which secularism attacks' as 'witnesses of man's need of God and allies in our quest of perfection' (Jones, 1928: 330). Put somewhat crudely, this view assumes that religion is the common property of mankind, that secularism is virtually identical with no-religion, and that the secularisation process therefore leads in every case out into the wilderness of unbelief.

But is the secularisation process irreversible? Most these days seem to be convinced that it is. Harvey Cox, as we have seen, called it 'almost certainly irreversible', and many would concur. Those who do so, however, are basing their opinions less on what they see happening than on what they want to happen, or are afraid may be happening. Developments in the opposite direction, away from the secular and toward the religious (and here we may simply recall the resurgence of conservative and pentecostal types of Christianity in various parts of the world, and the 'Islamic revolution' in Iran and Libya), do not suggest that the process is irreversible. In some cases it may be no more than a transitional stage through which religious belief and practice pass on their way to new positions. But here it is unsafe to generalise too far. The student's role, as I have already said, is to diagnose. What the ultimate prognosis may be, no one can tell.

In this matter of diagnosis, the secularisation debate thus far has been less than satisfactory. One reason for this has been a tendency to interpret religion in terms of only one of its four modes, that of intellectual 'belief', leaving aside or undervaluing its existential, social and ethical aspects.

It is striking that very many of those who argue about secularisation, and almost all of those who argue for it, take for granted that religion is in the last analysis a matter of 'things believed'. Science, they observe, has for centuries been contradicting, point by point, these beliefs. The cosmos has been emptied of its supernaturals. Religious explanations of natural events have been shown to be false. Natural explanations of religious events, on the other hand, have won the day – and where they have not, or where no such explanation has emerged, then so much the worse for religion. Surely, then, it is argued, 'modern man' has become an independent agent in the world, a free being who has been once and for all emancipated from the tutelage of the 'spiritual commonwealth'. Religion, they say, has 'lost its credibility' – a state of affairs to which religious communities are only too likely to respond by adjusting their message to what they suppose the 'common man' still needs that they are able to provide – usually ethical guidance.

But this is to shift the emphasis of religion from one of its modes (the intellectual) to another (the ethical). Why, in phenomenological terms, should the one be more important than the other? And what of the social mode? If one were to judge the rate of secularisation with reference to the incidence of attendance at acts of corporate worship, then it might well turn out to be the case that there is little to choose between 'secular' Sweden and 'religious' India. On the existential-intellectual axis, on the other hand, there would be no contest.

Here and there in recent discussion, there have been attempts to use terms like 'unbelief' and 'irreligion' to cover some of the same ground as that to which the secularisation discussion addresses itself. Neither is very satisfactory, however. From what I have just said, it must be clear that to speak in this way of 'unbelief' first of all presupposes that virtually the only thing that matters in the world of religion is what one believes; what one actually *does* is of comparatively little importance. But however typical this may be of post-Enlightenment ways of thinking about religion, it is in fact western and parochial, and corresponds hardly at all to the way in which non-western cultures function. Furthermore, it makes a great deal of difference, if 'unbelief' be accepted as a category, precisely *what* it is that is not believed. Intellectualisations in religion are highly variable things, and within even the most orthodox religion there may be considerable areas of 'unbelief'. These will however differ totally from one tradition to another. A Hindu atheist and a Christian atheist (to sharpen the language still further) are different, because they disbelieve in different gods. In Christian terms, the Buddhist is an atheist, but does this make of him an unbeliever?

'Unbelief' as an analytical category I therefore find entirely unsatisfactory, since it emphasises only one corner of the religious totality. Clearly one could not use parallel terms in respect of other modes of religion – 'religious misbehaviour' for instance, as the counterpart to 'religious behaviour', or 'immorality' in contrast to 'morality' (though in German it is possible to contrast *Glaube*, 'faith', with *Unglaube*, 'unfaith'). Nor is the secularisation process necessarily accompanied by 'unbelief': often belief in intellectual terms simply shifts sideways into another area, no less committed, no less social, no less ethical than what preceded it.

'Irreligion' is scarcely better placed, since again the word depends on some measure of clarity as to what actually constitutes religion in the first place. Colin Campbell rather gives the show away when he defines irreligion as '... those beliefs and actions which are expressive of attitudes of hostility or indifference *toward the prevailing religion* [my italics], together with indications of the rejection of its demands' (Campbell, 1972: 21). This is surely clear enough: that in these terms, 'irreligion' is as much a cultural as a genuinely religious antiphenomenon, and by no means involves the rejection of the possibilities of religion-as-such. To be sure, elsewhere Campbell describes the same phenomenon as 'relative' or 'specific' irreligion, and allows that it may be 'associated with attitudes of sympathy for other religions'; hence it is 'not uncommon to find secularists or humanists who speak favourably about Buddhism whilst condemning Christianity' (Campbell, 1972: 33). And in the first decade of the present century, Guyau made substantially the same point when he interpreted, in his classic *L'Irrêligion de l'avenir*, the decline of religion as being a decline in belief in ecclesiastical dogmas, and predicted that these would be replaced by alternative metaphysical hypotheses. One may perhaps conclude that *if* religion be interpreted in a 'culture-bound' way, then to shake one's fist at its local manifestations may seem to be a rejection of religion-as-such, but that there is no absolute reason why it should actually be so. Only when the question of the existence of the supernatural order (or perhaps 'the transcendent') has been answered in terms of a final and uncompromising denial, is it possible to speak of total irreligion.

If secularisation is a process, *involving* (though certainly not identical with) unbelief, the transfer of authority from 'religious' to 'secular' sources, and therefore a loosening of the bands which hold individuals together in companies of believers, how does the process begin and proceed?

Concerning beginnings, we may be brief, not because the matter is unimportant, but because the social and ideological causes of secularisation are fairly obvious. On the social level, the chief contributory factor has been the liberation of the individual from the necessity to maintain, as a member of a tribe or a tightly knit family, sacred custom, particularly as this relates to the powerful world of the spirits and the ancestors. In an agrarian community, ritual is maintained unbroken from generation to generation within the family. But once industrialisation and urbanisation set in, and more and more individuals are lumped together into anonymous urban communities, these links are broken, and religion either becomes the individual's private concern, or is neglected altogether. Add to this the spread of 'popular' education, in which the cause-and-effect categories of rational discourse are elevated above sacred tradition, and the gradual emergence of alternative ideologies, to which the individual may accommodate himself by his own free choice (and which in some cases may of course be anti-traditional), and the potential secularisation pattern is virtually complete. Instead of only one authority, which is that of the hierarchy of which the family is a part, and which extends over the whole of life, there are many authorities. Pragmatic concerns pass to groups and parties who conduct their affairs mostly without recourse to the supernatural order; what the individual does about his own immortal longings (if he has any) is his own concern, though a minimal and moralising 'civil religion' may be retained as a bastion against total moral collapse, and ancient supernatural war-gods may be brought out of retirement should the occasion arise (most recently, as far as the West was concerned, in 1914). The result may have little enough of pattern about it, but a very elementary shape emerges none the less.

It has three parts, three simultaneously emerging phenomena, which I shall call (a) rejection, (b) adaptation and (c) reaction. In contrast to some other theories of secularisation, this model has at least the virtue of simplicity. But I believe that it is comprehensive enough to meet most of the contingencies.

The phenomenon of rejection

On this point we may be fairly brief, since we have already covered a good deal of the ground. What is rejected is the right of a previously accepted authority to make any demands at all on the life of the individual, either in respect of what is to be believed, or what is to be done in consequence of that belief. If 'science' has shown up one part of a religious tradition as apparently untrustworthy, then it is concluded that in all else, science is equally to be believed. Religious traditions are not the revealed decrees of supernatural authorities, but the human products of ages gone by, produced in response to demands which no longer obtain and conditions which no longer exist. Although the phenomenon as such has made an immense impact on western thought since the eighteenth century, we may take an Indian example. Writing in his book *The Discovery of India*, Jawaharlal Nehru stated bluntly: 'We have got to get rid of that narrowing religious outlook, that obsession with the supernatural and metaphysical speculations, that loosening of the mind's discipline in religious ceremonial and mystical emotionalism, which come in the way of our understanding ourselves and the world' (Nehru, 1956: 552 f.).

Clearly in this case, 'science' is being put forward as a counter-authority to religion, and one may perhaps be tempted to conclude that *homo religiosus* is simply moving sideways and exchanging one type of priesthood for another. At least the secular ideologies which take the place of religious traditions contain a surprisingly large range of traditional religious ritual expressions – prophets, priests and kings, temples and shrines, pilgrimages and processions, holy scriptures, orthodoxies and heresies. But in one point there is a difference: the ultimate point of reference in the new secular ideology lies within the world, and not beyond it. The Marxist heaven is to be a classless society on earth, and the process of history is controlled not by supernatural, but by natural, forces. That not all those who reject religion are crypto-Marxists is clear enough; but at least it is evident that where religion is being replaced (and not merely leaving a total vacuum in the realm of ultimate meaning), the replacement is one of supernatural categories by natural. The gods have been banished from their sanctuaries, and nothing prevents these being made into museums, theatres or warehouses. To take another Indian example, it is not many years since the Government of India distributed a film entitled 'Temples of Tomorrow'. Its subject – hydro-electric power stations!

The phenomenon of adaptation

The 'liberal' position in religion has always caused a great deal of puzzlement to the opponents of religion, who generally assume (perhaps because they have read too many second-rate text books) that believers are either fundamentalists, orthodox or nothing. On the one hand, religious allegiance is often more a matter of orthopraxy (doing the right thing) than of orthodoxy (believing the right doctrines), and many traditions, such as the Hindu, give the individual almost unlimited freedom in questions of intellectual belief. But even where this is less true, the believer has considerable latitude in restating the implications of his religious allegiance in terms of what he otherwise knows about the world.

But 'restatement' is not necessary where the fundamentals of the faith have never been called in question. However, a sustained attack (for instance from the side of 'science') always leads, sooner or later, to an attempt at reconciliation. Where the points made by the scientists are (or appear to be) incontrovertible, the only question that matters is whether they do, or do not, touch the 'essence' of the religious affirmation.

In the secularisation process, the liberal position involves taking the attack seriously, allowing that the opponents of religion may be right up to a point, but insisting that when all allowances have been made, there remains an area of religion which emerges unscathed. This 'area' can then be developed afresh to meet the demands of changed conditions. Sarvepalli Radkhakrishnan put it this way:

> Leaders of Hindu thought and practice are convinced that the times require, not a surrender of the basic principles of Hinduism, but the restatement of them with special reference to the needs of a more complex and mobile social order (Radhakrishnan, 1960: 92).

Or as Charles Gore once wrote:

> ... if the true meaning of the [Christian] faith is to be made sufficiently conspicuous it needs disencumbering, reinterpreting, explaining (Gore, 1904: vii).

Similar statements could be assembled without difficulty from every major religious tradition.

This is not the place to describe in detail the emergent category of 'liberal religion', but three points may be made briefly.

The first is that it appears, not of its own accord, but in response to challenges from outside.

Secondly, it speaks frequently of 'the essence of religion', which usually consists, not of rituals or any other contingent externals, but of a set of ethical precepts based on the hypothesis of a moral Ultimate Reality.

Thirdly, it makes much use of the term 'universal religion', which it again usually conceives in terms of the same moral precepts, and regards as being distinguishable from the 'bibles and creeds and rubrics' with which religion has in the course of time surrounded itself. It argues that humanity is one, and stands in need of one code of practice, which on examination will be found to be either contained in the deliverances of a dominant tradition, or found as the 'golden core' of all traditions equally.

On the matter of whether the universal essence of religion is rational or non-rational, all that can be said in this connection is that opinions differ. Elsewhere I have written in some detail about the collision between these two intellectual possibilities – the one more rationally ethical, the other more experientially 'existential' (Sharpe, 1978). In either case, however, the 'universals' in question would not have emerged, without the impulse (or perhaps the irritation) of a body of secular opinion challenging the right of the traditional doctrines and outward manifestations of religion to command human allegiance.

In some situations, it may even be maintained by the representatives of the great religions themselves that the secularisation process is the best thing which could have happened to them. It has cleared away masses of useless and outworn garbage, and has focussed attention on what is essential – the place of mankind in the world, the *saeculum.* Such attempts are always seriously meant, though one cannot always avoid the sense of desperation which attends some of them. Writings of this kind were somewhat common in the late 1960s. Today they are decidedly uncommon, perhaps because they were equivocal about the ultimate life-and-death issues, and commanded little support.

The phenomenon of reaction

Faced with powerful attacks from the direction of 'science' or 'politics', and with nervous attempts on the part of liberals to achieve relevance at any price, there almost always emerges a third force, rallying round the flag of 'the faith once and for all delivered to the saints'. These are the 'conservatives' or the 'fundamentalists', who claim to be representing the true faith, but who are in most cases restating a position in extreme polemical terms over against both those who have rejected it and those who have tried to adapt it.

If we use the term 'fundamentalism' to refer, not to a particular school of thought within Protestant Christianity, but to the utterly uncompromising adherence to any precisely formulated (usually scriptural) tradition, then it may be claimed without much exaggeration that fundamentalism always emerges in response to a previously existing liberalism. It is in other words just as much a product of the secularisation process as is the liberalism it attempts to abolish. In Christian terms, fundamentalism dates from the period just before the First World War, when there appeared a series of twelve pamphlets entitled *The Fundamentals: A Testimony to the Truth* (1911ff.). Although their main emphasis was on the infallibility of the Bible, they condemned a wide range of 'Christian deviations' – 'Modernism' or 'liberalism' (by which they meant the application of evolutionary theory and higher criticism to the study of the Bible), Roman Catholicism, Mormonism and Christian Science among them. It seemed to the writers that to disturb any one stone in the biblical edifice was tantamount to destroying the whole:

> Let us then, by repudiating this modern criticism, show our condemnation of it. What does it offer us? Nothing. What does it take away? Everything. Do we have any use for it? No!

As the secularisation process continued, the fundamentalist voice became more and more strident. It came to a notable climax in America in connection with the celebrated 'monkey trial' of 1925 (in which a Tennessee schoolteacher, J.T. Scopes, was prosecuted for teaching evolutionism), since when it has passed through various phases, depending – as might be expected – on the relative strength of secular and liberal forces at any given time. Others of its enemies have included 'godless communism' (representing phase one of the secularisation process), a 'politicised' World Council of Churches (representing phase two), as well as the relaxed moral standards of society as a whole, which are attributed to the cumulative effects of both overt godlessness and desperate (and culpable) liberal attempts to make common cause with the values of 'the world'.

Other comparable expressions of the same process include the emergence of minority groups (commonly called 'cults' or 'sects') which again have rejected both the dominant values of secular society and the compromises of the major religious bodies in face of those values. One cannot easily generalise about sects, which (not least in our day) exhibit a bewildering variety of attitudes and practices. Most, however, have arisen as expressions of the desire for the renewal of absolute values and absolute standards in religion. Clearly they would not be needed if such absolutes were always observed in the major religious bodies. As it is, the further the secularisation process moves on one wing of popular opinion, the more competing sects may be expected to arise, all bent on the same thing phenomenologically – the re-asserting of the need for complete acceptance of a total religious authority, and the rejection of all opposing or half-way measures.

Authority is the key word in this process. The basic question is always 'What, in ultimate questions, is it absolutely necessary to believe?' Or alternatively, 'In what or whom is it possible to place absolute trust?' Where the answer is formulated in terms of a scripture – the Bible, the Qur'an, the Veda – we speak more or less automatically of 'fundamentalism'. But equally the final source of authority may be a person – a prophet, an interpreter, a seer, a guru – who may or may not expound scripture in traditional terms, but who is always believed by his or her followers to stand in a special relationship to ultimate reality, and therefore to be supremely authoritative in all matters having to do with the life of the spirit. In either case, however, the process is commonly one of *restoration* of that which has been challenged, and which has fallen into disuse and neglect. As such, the process is not new. The Buddha claimed to have rediscovered the eternal *dhamma* (law) which, like an ancient city overgrown by the jungle, has been lost and forgotten. Jesus of Nazareth asserted that he had come, not to destroy but to fulfil (to bring to completion) the law and the prophets of Israel (Matthew 5:17). Muhammad proclaimed the pure worship and the sovereignty of Allah over against the polytheistic accretions which had obscured them. Similar – though hardly equally convincing – claims have subsequently been made by and on behalf of a vast number of new prophets, messiahs and gurus. In our day it is easy to see how the secularisation process has opened the way to more and more such claimants. Given a certain climate of religious opinion in the West, in which total religious indifference has reached epidemic proportions, and in which numerically strong religious bodies are side-stepping more and more of the basic life-and-death issues of human life while insisting more and more shrilly on standards of ethical conduct for their own sake, attempts at the restoration of basics are likely to become more and more numerous.

The phenomenon of reaction, however, is not limited to the geographical West, though some writers still tend to treat it in mainly Western terms. The recent history of Hindu India is full of 'reaction movements' – among them the Arya Samaj (out of which most others have developed: it dates from 1875), the Hindu Mahasabha, the Rashtriya Swayamsevak Sangh (RSS) and the Jana Sangh. Here the practical emphases have included the 'reconversion' of ex-Hindus *from* Islam and Christianity *to* the Hindu fold; the forbidding of cow-slaughter, the maintenance of caste law, which is prescribed by certain Hindu scriptures and which the constitution of India rejects; and the establishment of a Sanskrit-based language (Hindi) as the official language of the whole of India. Here the phenomena which are being reacted against are partly foreign, partly political, partly liberal Hindu, partly secular and 'scientific' in the style of Jawaharlal Nehru. Affirmations are socially conservative and politically authoritarian and rest on the foundations of the total and unquestioned authority of the Vedic scriptures as a spiritual, legal and political source. Other religions are permitted to exist in the programmes of these movements (none of which has ever acquired sufficient political muscle to be able to put them into operation, let it be said); they are not on the other hand permitted to convert, or even to attempt to convert, Hindus.

Much the same combination of religious, political and social factors is observable in the case of the recent Islamic resurgence in Iran, Libya and Pakistan. In every case the intrusive factor has been Western commerce, culture and religion, which has brought about 'stage one' in the secularisation process. Some evidence of 'stage two' (Islamic Modernism) there has also been, though on a fairly modest scale. But the 'Islamic revolution', with all its odd alliances, has been a fully-fledged reassertion of absolute values in respect of the Qur'an and its interpreters, and of traditional standards in respect of law, public morals, dress and the like. That the outward impression has also been strongly anti-Western is perhaps only to be expected, bearing in mind the fact that the new and implicitly anti-Islamic forces earlier this century came out of the geographical West.

As a final example we may perhaps cite the plethora of 'new religious movements' which in recent years have emerged in Japan and Korea – both of them countries on which war has left deep scars, in which traditional values have been called in question and in which liberalism has simply not had the power to reshape shattered societies and inject a sense of purpose into the popular mind. In many cases the new movements have been strongly authoritarian and explicitly political, as well as re-asserting the traditional values of a society threatened by the forces of rapid social change.

*

The process of secularisation, we may perhaps conclude, is by no means a one-way movement. On the contrary, it is a three-way process, no one part of which is more important than the totality. Although a great deal of attention has inevitably been paid to its latest and most spectacular manifestations, there is absolutely no sense in which the process as such is a new one, and we have no reason whatever to suppose that the process is an irreversible one. It is an important, and in some senses even a dominant, aspect of present-day religious life; that we may assert. What we may not do, on the other hand, is to predict that the contingencies of the present will last indefinitely, or that the present line of development can be projected into the indefinite future. Already history has shown how often periods of decline in religious observance have been followed by periods of revival and the re-assertion of old values, and there is no reason to assume that the tensions of the present day are anything more than new variations on an age-old human theme.

Let the student, therefore, be conscientious in reading the signs and assembling evidence, but careful in the extreme when it comes to predicting the ultimate direction in which developments are tending. Futurology is a pleasant (though at times a disturbing) exercise, and short-term predictions can sometimes be made with a fair degree of certainty. But the study of religion has this advantage among many, that it has a habit of cutting futurologists down to size. No human process is irreversible; while if God is involved in the human process at all, it is surely unwise to set bounds to what he may or may not do with his creation. In our day, secularisation is a fact, because religion is a fact. As an action, it produces a reaction – it has always been so, and it will always be so. In sociological or psychological terms, we may argue about it how we will. The religious issue is still that stated almost two thousand years ago by a

Christian writer who may or may not have been the Apostle Peter:

> First of all you must understand this, that scoffers will come in the last days with scoffing, following their own passions and saying, 'Where is the promise of his coming? For ever since the fathers fell asleep, all things have continued as they were from the beginning of creation.' ... But according to his promise we wait for new heavens and a new earth in which righteousness dwells. (2 Peter 3:3, 4, 13).

Nine
Religions and Cultures

In considering the process by which religious authority comes to be transferred to or taken over by secular agencies and organisations, we have to some extent sidestepped another very important question, namely, how what we call 'religion' is related to what we call 'culture'. To judge by the regularity with which one hears and reads about 'culture' in today's media, the question of precisely what constitutes 'culture' or 'a culture' ought to be in everyone's mind. But this is hardly the case. In matters cultural, exact analysis is very much a matter for the experts (principally anthropologists and sociologists), while on the popular level, the word is used to refer to a variety of things, from the arts on the one hand to national identity on the other, and to many areas in between. There are therefore numerous pitfalls in the way of an understanding of how religion and culture are related. So much depends on the shade of meaning which we give to these two words.

If, for instance, we narrow down religion to its existential mode, claiming it to be entirely a matter of the individual's relationship on the spiritual plane with the power which created and which governs the universe, then there is no particularly compelling reason why religion ('essential' religion, that is) should have any cultural dimension at all. The Supreme Reality is presumably above such matters altogether. Certainly symbols of some kind are needed if the believer is not to be completely inarticulate in face of the final mystery; but any attempt to say that the Real is in any way dependent on those symbols will be stoutly resisted precisely because of the degree to which symbol-systems are known to be culturally conditioned. The greater part of religious opinion has indeed always refused to admit (or perhaps recognise) that what it believes, says and does rests in any way on the shifting sands of culture: not only is the core of the message to the world eternal; so too are all but the most trivial of the ways in which it is transmitted.

On the opposite wing of opinion are those who maintain with equal force that nothing – or at least nothing that is observable – in religion can be separated from the cultural forms in which it expresses itself. Every last detail – every idea, every ritual, every need met, every controversy, every organisation – has arisen out of the needs and concerns of a specific culture and must be viewed in that light. But this point having once been made, opinions may then vary. For some, it may be taken as conclusive proof that the whole of religion is a human contrivance having no 'eternal dimension' at all. Others accept the fact – indeed the inevitability – of cultural dependence without necessarily relinquishing the view that there remains a vastly important core or essence to religion to which the cultural forms point, but which they by no means exhaust. Either way, it is not uncommon at the present time to find religionists saying that culture-free religion has always been a mirage, and that unless religion learns to come to terms with the cultural factor, it will never understand itself, and will have no hope of making any impression on any human community. But before we proceed further, we must look a little more closely at the operative word 'culture'.

It is almost as difficult to arrive at an adequate definition of culture as it is of religion. In a 1960 article Albert C. Cafagna quoted a large number of sociological definitions, most of which had at least this much in common, that they saw culture as a type of learned behaviour, a matter of 'transmitted social learning', involving the passing on of ideas by various means – verbal, symbolical, imitation, and so on. Ideas are therefore of central importance. With this, we may compare the German encyclopaedia (Brockhaus, 1970) definition of *Kultur* as '... the totality of typical life-forms of a community, including its spiritual/intellectual system [*Geistesverfassung*], and especially its scale of values.'

We must however remember that cultures are no more static than are religions, and that they must not be approached as though they were fixed, permanently formed entities, each having its own immutable shape and content. Much trouble has been caused in the past by the failure of students of religion to appreciate the processes of religious change; to add to this a failure to recognise cultural change will inevitably darken counsel still further.

To speak of culture therefore should involve both the notion of growth (as in laboratory cultures) and the notion of cohesion within definable boundaries. But in this present case, working definitions are of relatively little use without some knowledge of how and where the word arose, and the ways in which it has come to be coupled with religion. We must therefore take a moment to inquire into a little of its past history.

At times, dictionaries of quotations have their uses. H.L. Mencken's *A New Dictionary of Quotations* (1942) contains under the heading 'Culture' nothing earlier than 1827 – a passage in which the Scottish Germanophile Thomas Carlyle describes the 'great law of culture':

> Let each become all that he was created capable of being; expand, if possible, to his full growth; resisting all impediments, casting off all foreign, especially all noxious adhesions ...

When the German word *Kultur* (once spelt *Cultur*) entered the intellectual life of Europe early in the nineteenth century, it was in the high years of the Romantic movement, with all its visions of unique personal integrity; but it was also at a time when attempts were being made to shape a new, unified Germany out of a large number of independent states, of which Prussia was the largest and most powerful. What was needed to hold these states together? A unified administration, clearly, with all its government offices and national institutions. But beyond this, it was still more necessary to try to convince Germans that they *were* Germans, and not, say, Prussians or Bavarians. On some levels this proved well-nigh impossible; but the university-trained intellectuals seized upon the word *Kultur* to express their ideal of a nation bound together by a common history, common attitudes and loyalities, united under one law and one Emperor, and pure, having cast off what Carlyle called 'all foreign ... [and] noxious adhesions'.

To some extent, this was tribalism writ large, and the spectre of Antisemitism was looming on the horizon. Primal societies differ from this pattern in size rather than in kind. And as in primal societies, the supernaturals who sustain the life of the people had to be acknowledged as part of the cultural totality: 'For all the peoples walk each in the name of its god, but we will walk in the name of the Lord our God for ever and ever' (Micah 4:5). Pass beyond the boundaries of the nation (or the culture) and you must expect to find other languages spoken, other laws observed – and other gods worshipped. Conflict between nations was also conflict between their supernatural protectors – a tribal pattern last seen in unrestricted operation on the battlefields of Europe in 1914-1918. Without this supernatural point of reference, much religious thought in the late nineteenth and early twentieth centuries decreed that no culture was complete. German culture involved at some point the idea of the German God (*der deutsche Gott*) who sustained and inspired it, and who in the trenches of Flanders confronted the effete God of the French, the easy-going businessman-God of the English and the pragmatic God of the Americans.

However – to continue the history of ideas line a little further – in the English-speaking world of earlier this century, the English word 'culture' had already begun to be identified, not with society as a whole, but with its intellectual and aesthetic forms of expression. 'Culture is properly described as the love of perfection; it is a study of perfection,' wrote Matthew Arnold in 1869; four years later, in his *Literature and Dogma*, he was to define culture, after a fashion, as being 'to know the best that has been said and thought in the world'. But already a gap was opening up between what the secular world regarded as intellectually or aesthetically 'the best', and what much of the western religious world regarded as *morally* the best. An aesthetic 'best' might well be at war with a religious 'best', and vice versa: religion and culture were coming apart – a point made starkly by one J.G. Holland in 1876 when he wrote that '[a]s culture comes in, faith goes out'. This most Germans certainly did not believe, preferring the view that without its unique faith, there could be no culture worthy of the name.

Leaving aesthetics aside, in its nationalist sense earlier this century culture was not so much a measurable commodity as a set of ideas which served to set up boundaries between 'the people' (*das Volk*) and the rest of the world, 'the lesser breeds without the law', the barbarians or whatever. As we have said, its constituent elements included – as well as religion – geography, history, language, music, art and architecture; and its forms of expression ranged all the way from ethical and moral values to jokes.

As far as the study of religion was concerned, these theories had one another important consequence. Having recognised the role of religion in one's own culture, intellectual honesty demanded the recognition that other cultures, too, might see things in precisely the same way. Already there were a number of parts of the world in which Hindus, Muslims and others were resisting the religious and commercial encroachments of the West partly by arguing that their religion (in India, chiefly Hinduism) was attuned to the natural environment and needs of India in a way that western Christianity was not. Indeed, in the years before the First World War there was a far-reaching alliance between Indian nationalism and Hindu revivalism, and many Hindus were already arguing in terms of the importance of Hinduism to India's cultural heritage. But so too were a growing number of western scholars, particularly those who for other reasons held a low view of Christian missions. During the First World War, a further sensitive issue was Christian Germany's alliance with Muslim Turkey (causing one English propagandist to write scornfully about 'Deutschland über Allah'!) – paralleled by Britain's use of Hindu, Muslim and Sikh troops. Small wonder, perhaps, that the western nations as a whole were forced in these years into an (at least temporary) attitude of greater respect for cultural diversity, cultural integrity and the inadvisability of interfering too much with existing patterns of religion and culture in non-Christian countries. But politics aside, more and more liberal students of religion were coming to the conclusion that each individual culture should be permitted to find its own level of faith and devotion. This was what the German theologian Ernst Troeltsch meant in the 1920s when he wrote, in his last, posthumously-published book, that Christianity is of a piece with European culture: '... our whole Christianity is indissolubly bound up with elements of the ancient and modern civilisations of Europe ... We cannot live without a religion, yet the only religion we can endure is Christianity' (Troeltsch, 1923: 128).

Equally, to attempt to transplant a religion (any religion) into alien soil was, in Troeltsch's opinion, doomed to failure. A religion grows only in a certain soil and a certain climate. Separate it from that environment, and the results may be fatal: 'There can be no conversion or transformation of one [great religion] into the other, but only a measure of agreement and of mutual understanding' (ibid.: 130).

*

What Troeltsch was saying in the early 1920s sounds very familiar in today's climate of opinion, and it is salutary to reflect that ideas of this order have such a long history in western religious thought. But whereas the cultural theorists of the earlier part of the century were arguing from a position of strength (or at least pride), today's debaters more often argue from a position of considerable disillusionment with western culture and religion. It is urged that an infusion of either into the lives of non-western nations is bound to be culturally harmful; that it has been harmful in the past, and will inevitably be so in the future. It is further argued that to the extent that existing religious traditions reflect the cultural values of the people (any people), they are fulfilling a necessary and important task, and should be left to continue to do so in their own way, without an outside religious interference which may be no more than colonialism in disguise.

As this last point shows, today's argument has a sizeable political component, and touches upon matters on which feelings run high. It is however no part of my present purpose to supply ammunion for use on this particular battlefield. Instead I shall try to map out some of the ways in which religion and culture may interrelate, in the hope of being able to show that the student is in fact faced with a range of possibilities requiring evaluation.

As I have tried to show throughout this book, religion is not a simple thing, nor does it fulfil only one function. Depending on the emphases and priorities of different times and places, as well as on the inclinations of individuals, it may be more personal or more collective, more supportive or more criticial of social organisations, more 'priestly' or more 'prophetic' (I shall return to this distinction shortly). If we take 'culture' to be a shorthand term denoting the overall value system operative within a definable human community, and the ways in which that system expresses itself, then religion may serve to bolster and extend that system; or it may do precisely the opposite. And without an examination of each case separately, there is no way of determining which it will be. Further, we have to be constantly on our guard against falling into the trap of assuming that cultures will always remain enclosed within tidy geographical or ethnic boundaries. If a culture is, among other things, the human embodiment of a specific value-system, all we can say is that however things may have been in the past in some parts of the world, today's global scene could scarcely be untidier. Today there are two or three would-be 'cosmo-cultures' – aggressively expansive value-systems, each of which believes profoundly in itself and in its own ideals – in interplay with multitudes of the displaced and dismembered fragments of yesterday's local cultures, most of which feel profoundly threatened by the cosmocultures and what they stand for. Where the cosmocultures have some religious (or for that matter anti-religious) point of reference, then the threatened members of each minority group separately will affirm their own identity with the help of their traditional religious symbols and values. This will not be the only means used: obviously political and economic values are of vast importance, and will often be dominant; but the religious factor may in the end prove to be the most tenacious, and the one most easily identified, as well as being the easiest to blame when something goes wrong. An obvious example would be Northern Ireland, where two communities (which elsewhere in the world might well have been called cultures) are separated by politics, economics and history, as well as by the religious allegiance which almost everyone identifies as the main dividing factor.

Previously we have talked about four modes in which religion functions – the existential, intellectual, social and ethical dimensions which serve as a mimimum check-list for the student seeking an overall view of religion. It was never intended that this list should in any way exhaust the possibilities, particularly since each mode can in any given instance appear in a negative, as well as a positive, sense. Religion may be intellectual or anti-intellectual, social or anti-social. It may also approach the culture in which it finds itself in either an affirmative or a negative way, either supporting or attempting to overthrow (or at least modify) the values it finds there. Often in practice the former attitude will be linked with the *priestly*, and the latter with the *prophetic* role among believers and functionaries. In general, the priestly represents the conservative, culture-supportive attitude, while the prophetic function is radical and culture-critical.

Illustrating this distinction from the biblical tradition, there the prophet is one who comes with a message from God, in a particular situation, to an individual or a community. His message may be one of encouragement, hope, warning, or judgment; it may be well received, or it may not; his words may be solicited, or they may come altogether unbidden. His constant concern is to pass on a message which he believes has come direct from God. His constant refrain is 'Thus says the Lord.' The prophet is a radical, in the sense that he is constantly seeking to penetrate to the root (*radix*) of religion in the faithful observance of God's requirements to do justice, love mercy and show humility in face of the Divine. His business is with words and symbolic actions; his chief weapon is insistent eloquence; and he is utterly impatient of anything which he feels to stand in the way of divine truth. A prophet, therefore, is always more or less at odds with culture, and culture may treat him harshly. In a negative sense, culture produces him; but it never welcomes him. His emergence is wholly incalculable. Like any genius, he is apt to arise out of the most umpromising surroundings, without warning, without preparation. And he may disappear again, leaving no disciples and no successors. Should he find disciples, these may come to venerate the man more than his message; while those who reach an accommodation with their culture are liable in the long run to be called 'false prophets' for their pains. The true prophet is always unique; as C.H. Dodd has said, '[w]e may study the antecedents and environment of the prophet, and account for the direction his genius took; but just that unique quality that makes him a prophet evades our definition ... Each is an individual, with the incalculable originality which is the inseparable mark of genius' (Dodd, 1947: 26f.). Faced with a prophet, those who are secure within a culture and its values may react in various ways. They may accept him, reject him or ignore him; but sooner or later they must note the challenge which he poses to their value-system – that is, to the roots of the culture to which they belong.

If the prophet is the genuine radical, summoning a people to penitence, renewal and action, the priest will more often be the genuine conservative, calling upon his people to follow along the true line of sacred tradition. His strength is in the continuity he represents; his authority in his position as a consistent and reliable mediator between God and man. His business is with prayer, ritual, liturgy, worship, not as ends in themselves (though human nature being what it is, any or all may of course become ends in themselves), but as a means of approach to the Holy God: 'True instruction was in his mouth, and no wrong was found upon his lips. He walked with me in peace and uprightness, and he turned many from iniquity. For the lips of a priest should guard knowledge, and men should seek instruction from his mouth, for he is the messenger of the Lord of hosts' (Malachi 2: 6f. – a prophetic assessment of what a priest ought to be at a time when many priests were not living up to these ideals).

Prophet and priest; preacher and celebrant; radical and conservative; renewal and the maintenance of tradition – the tension between the two has been fairly constant in the world of religion. The priest, whose very existence is bound up with the right exercise of his sacred function in society, is apt to condemn the prophet's lack of formal education, his crudity, and his disrespect for properly constituted authority. The prophet denounces what he holds to be the priest's preoccupation with externals, his conscious endeavour to perpetuate the past by ritual re-presentation, his natural conservatism and distaste for change, and much else besides. 'I hate, I despise your feasts, and I take no delight in your solemn assemblies ... But let justice roll down like waters, and righteousness like an ever-flowing stream' (Amos 5: 21, 24). Frequently, the priestly and the prophetic minds fail completely to understand – or even to try to understand – each other's position.

Now clearly in the history of religion there have been false prophets and renegade priests, as well as priests who were prophets and prophets who were also priests. But the *types* are generally recognisable; and each has its cultural function. These functions are, however, by no means constant.

On the one hand, final responsibility for the carrying out of rituals and the making and administrating of a culture's laws often rests in one and the same person – a chieftain, king or emperor, who as well as being supreme ruler and law-maker is also high priest. It is in this connection that scholars speak of 'sacral kingship', meaning by it that the chieftain-king-emperor (and those whom he chooses to appoint) carries out the two-way function of representing the people before God (or the gods) and Gods to the people. Between the natural and supernatural orders he is *pontifex maximus* – the supreme mediator. Certainly he may build, as the Pharaoh Akhenaton tried to build, new bridges and channels of communication to new gods: but he does so at infinite risk, since most believe that 'where it is not necessary to change, it is necessary not to change'. As a rule, should he fail to maintain the rituals and the sacrifices, or cause the channels of communication to become blocked, he is deposed and his functions are taken over by some other ruler. Similarly, should his armies lose in battle, this too may be taken as a sign, that his priestly duties are not being carried out properly (an ancient principle which perhaps last operated in the case of Kaiser Wilhelm

II of Germany in 1919). As well as the outcome of battle, drought, famine and disease may also serve as signs of failure on this level.

With the disappearance from the West of feudal society, the sacral kingship, too, gradually disappeared – though some few of its symbols still survive here and there. In other parts of the world, for instance in certain Islamic countries, more remains, and the Ayatollah Khomeini of Iran is probably the closest approximation to the traditional priest-king presently operating in the arena of world affairs. And yet in terms of our secularisation pattern, the Ayatollah represents the final (reaction) stage in the conflict of religious and secular authority, since his calling he sees as the *restoration* of traditional Islamic society rather than its simple maintenance.

It is the secularisation process which in fact provides the necessary key by which the student may hope to interpret the 'religion and culture' question. For as secularisation advances, cultures become more and more fragmented and unstable; old authorities are challenged; mobility increases; functions previously performed by religion (education, medicine, some degree of political control, the transmission of unquestioned values) are shifted to newer, secular agencies; priest-kings are replaced by constitutional monarchs or elected representatives; decisions are arrived at (at least in theory) by popular consensus. Religion, then, becomes only one part of the totality we call culture, but very often an isolated part which, however hard it may try to maintain contact with other parts of the totality, often fails precisely because those who run the remainder have either lost touch with the world of religion altogether or view it too narrowly.

In the Western world, the cause of this has rested in no small measure in the hands of religion's own people. This is not the place to argue the point in detail. We may merely say that to the extent to which the West has come to interpret religion more or less exclusively in moral terms (a result of a process traceable back to Kant and the Enlightenment), it has abandoned – or been forced out of – others of the interconnected mansions of culture. The process began in the late eighteenth century among Western intellectuals; a century later it was well under way; and by the last quarter of the twentieth century, it is virtually complete, at least in what we might call the religious mainstream. The claim that western culture rests on the foundations of the Judaeo-Christian religious tradition (just as Indian culture depends upon the Hindu tradition) is therefore a half-truth. It is true that western culture and western religion were once two aspects of one undivided whole (or at least of one interrelated complex). Today they have all too frequently been transmuted into two blurred and twisted faces, scowling at each other across a gulf of mutual misunderstanding and acrimony. Elsewhere in the world, where the secularisation process is less far advanced, the conflict is perhaps less marked; but it is almost always there in some form.

*

It cannot escape the student's attention that the claim that religion should once more become attuned to the value-systems of a specific culture always conceals certain assumptions. The first of these is that mainstream, establishment religion may be assumed accurately to represent the values of the cultural establishment. This is very seldom altogether true, and in western countries it is liable to be altogether false. Western cultures in our day seldom relate in any but the most casual and perfunctory fashion to their corresponding religious bodies. The second assumption is that the religious and cultural values being discussed are actually under threat: where the 'attunement' claim is made, it is almost always on behalf of some threatened minority whose collective identity is in danger of being submerged under what are trumpeted as being the false values of what we have called the cosmoculture. It is very seldom heard in respect of the values of a secure and powerful majority. In this case, it would seem that in part at least, the relationship between religion and culture is being used in order to further certain sectional interests.

Previously we quoted Ernst Troeltsch on the subject of the inseparability of Christianity and European culture. However convincing this judgment may have seemed in the earlier part of the twentieth century, it hardly stands up to close analysis, particularly if it be extended into a general principle. Buddhism originated in India, and was nourished on Indian soil for many centuries. Today its chief centres of influence are countries like Sri Lanka, Thailand and Japan. Islam, with its romantic image of *Arabia Felix*, the empty spaces and the loneliness of the vast desert, has actually owed relatively little to its country of origin, but has left its mark on some very remote places indeed, not least China, East and West Africa,

India and South-East Asia. And what of Christianity? Originating in Palestine, and shaped in the Hellenistic world by a combination of Jewish fervour, Greek thought and Roman law, it only assumed its modern shape in post-Enlightenment Europe and America. To this it is also necessary to add that since Troeltsch's day, the cultural focal points of Christianity have been steadily shifting away from Europe and North America, and toward what we now call the 'third world'.

Purely from the historical evidence, it is obvious that religious traditions have always been remarkably culturally mobile. None of the major traditions has been static for very long at a time. Sets of cultural values have been sometimes accepted, sometimes rejected, sometimes shunned, sometimes patronised. Religions on the move from one cultural setting to another have acquired and shed material on the way, to such an extent that there may in the end remain little enough to recall their original point of departure. In Christianity's case, the road from Calvary to Canterbury or California has been a long and hard road.

Religious traditions move from one cultural setting to another along a number of different channels. Five may be identified – migration, trade, imitation, conquest and mission. In some of these, the transmission of culture will be simple and automatic: a group of migrants, for instance, will take with them everything they can carry that reminds them of their origins and will often preserve these things tenaciously, at least for several generations. Thus what we today call 'ethnic religion' may be culturally as well as religiously a virtual carbon copy of conditions in the homeland. Where conquest is the determining factor, it is not uncommon to find a distinction arising between the religious and cultural forms which it is prudent for the conquered to assume in public and those which they observe in private – in the Roman Empire, for instance, where public religion was that of the Roman state, while the private religion (which the Romans called *superstitio*) remained local and virtually unclassifiable. Those who acquire their religion from elsewhere by imitation – and here we may perhaps cite the 'neo-Hindu' movements in the modern West – take only as much of the original religio-cultural totality as they think they need. This may be minimal, as in the case of the Transcendental Meditation movement of the Maharishi Mahesh Yogi; or it may appear to be almost total, as in the case of the International Society for Krishna

Consciousness, with its Indian food, dress and rituals. But even here the cultural imitation is superficial, and is bound to remain so until such time as Krishna's Western devotees acquire greater facility in Indian languages – which at present very few show any sign of even wanting to do.

The 'cultural' question, however, will always arise in its most acute form in connection with deliberate missionary activity. Do the 'missionary religions' (and for the Western student, that means mainly Christianity) set out to transmit specific cultural values as part of their total message? And if they do, will this not inevitably mean that they are deliberately bent on destroying cultures which they neither understand nor appreciate? A great many people in our day believe that this has actually happened, whether deliberately or not; that it ought never to have happened; and that everything possible should be done to prevent it ever happening again. Needless to say, these are emotive issues, in the midst of which the student may find it the hardest thing in the world to steer an analytical course.

Let us first of all recall, however, that cultural theory is a latecomer on the Western intellectual scene, and that its period of currency has coincided precisely with the period during which Western Christian missions have been most powerful, and Western influence on the world at large most marked. A century ago, there was absolutely no question about it: most Christian missionary agencies did see it as their sacred duty to transmit not only the message which had been entrusted to them, but also the social and cultural values which their nations had embraced. But – and this is important – they did not draw the sharp distinction between 'religion' on the one hand and 'culture' on the other which comes so naturally to the last quarter of the twentieth century. To be sure, German intellectuals had a great deal to say about the values of German *Kultur*, toward which they believed (naively but sincerely) the world as a whole was moving. But this did not mean that other 'cultural heritages' were to be thrown away as so much outmoded rubbish. Each on the contrary was to be studied assiduously with a view to finding which of its elements might perchance find a place in the *Kultur* of the future. The British and Americans for their part theorised less, and were less concerned with the abstractions which preoccupied the Germans: most of their Christian missionaries were less well educated than were the continentals, and were as a rule content mainly to transmit their Christian message as they had themselves received it, with all the symbols and forms of expression which a later age so unhesitatingly identifies as 'cultural' and therefore unessential. At times, the culturally aware and the culturally naive could arrive at diametrically opposite evaluations of what they encountered on the mission field.

The best example of this known to me is a difference of opinion which arose in the middle years of the nineteenth century among Christian missionaries working in India on the subject of the Hindu institution of caste. Here the controversy was precisely between German Lutherans, who saw caste as a social, cultural institution having religious overtones; and British missionaries belonging to various churches, but who all saw caste as a religious institution which apparently denied the idea of the universal brotherhood of man. Accordingly the British demanded of every convert that all overt caste practices should be publicly rejected as a mark of religious seriousness, while the Germans were prepared for the time being to allow many of these same practices to continue undisturbed. That it was the British (and later the American) view which won the day has often in subsequent years been advanced by critics as a prime example of cultural insensitivity on the missionaries' part. And so it was, in a way. But at the same time it was an example of what happens when a pre-secular situation (in which religion and culture are not separated the one from the other) is approached by two groups of observers who assume there to be a difference between the two, but who approach the same body of evidence from opposite angles. One saw it in terms of one analytical abstraction (culture), the other as another analytical abstraction (religion). Both were equally right – and equally wrong.

It could be argued – and it has been argued – that in taking a hard line against the institution of caste, the Anglo-Saxon missionaries in India were cutting themselves off from the most important cultural institution in the whole of Hindu India. And that in order to be capable of flourishing in Indian soil, Christianity would have to show much more social and cultural flexibility that it has shown hitherto. As it is, many a potential convert to Christianity in India (and of course elsewhere) has turned away from the Christian message, not on account of anything to do with religious truth or falsehood, but because it has seemed to demand of him that he part company with his own cultural heritage, of which Hinduism is such an integral part. Whether, as Mahatma Gandhi at one time supposed, becoming a Christian meant that the Hindu would be compelled to eat beef, drink liquor, speak English in all situations, revile the faith of his fathers, and wear funny clothes, we may be permitted to doubt. But it certainly appeared to the Hindu in that light for a great deal of the time. And Christians for their part for many years failed to realise the extent to which their religion had come to be identified with the intrusive culture and political apparatus of the West. Nor until very recently did they realise that their own secularisation process was leading, among other things, to the once-and-for-all separation of elements of culture – education, hospitals, the written word, and much else – from the religion with which it was once unconsciously identified.

In a pre-secular society, final authority in all areas of life rests (or is believed to rest) on the divine decree through which the chief, king or emperor rules, on which the laws are based, the seasonal rituals are carried out, and by which all human relations are regulated. To this authority, all the elements of culture are subservient: 'religion' and 'culture' are one and the same, religious on the vertical plane, cultural on the horizontal, but neither understandable without the other. But once the secularisation process has set in, and final authority is seen on the everyday level as resting not in divine decree but on a mixture of the testimony of experts and democratic consensus, then 'religion' may be what is left when all the 'cultural' elements in society have assumed an independent life of their own, or else a moral (and in some cases ritual) residue which has been allowed to retain control of the sanctuary, and which may in the end help to create well-behaved citizens.

Does this, then, mean that talk of a 'golden core' of religion, which has no intrinsic relationship with separate cultures, is merely wishful thinking? In very many cases, one is indeed forced to some such conclusion. Perhaps there are visionaries whose visions bear no relation to any existing world of symbols and values; but if there are, it is hard to see how they could ever communicate what they have experienced to any other human being. And even notions of what constitutes the 'essence' of religion are always formulated with reference to existing value-systems, and to what has come to be regarded as important and unimportant respectively in the lives of individuals and the cultures of which they are (however unwillingly) part. Claims that one or other religious tradition is 'universal' and therefore capable of being embraced by all human beings everywhere, though they may be accompanied by an acknowledgment that *some* of its elements are culturally conditioned and need to be cleared away, almost always in the last resort fall back on a moral core which is not open to negotiation, but which is at the same time part of an inherited value-system. Historically speaking, every would-be 'universal' religion has always proved on closer examination to be at the same time a highly specific, and often quite intransigent, particular religion, each with its own unique cultural component. To this rule, not even Baha'i or the Theosophical Society are exceptions.

We have mentioned the present-day claim that religion ought to be 'contextualised', that is, adapted to the value-systems which are natural to the part of the world and the culture within which it intends, or hopes, to operate. Now this is basically a piece of *missionary* strategy: it is after all very little use giving people answers to religious questions which they have never asked, couched in terms which they do not understand. Further, it seems that this theory was in part devised to account for two things: first, the lack of impact of the Christian message in some parts of the post-colonial world (including most of the old 'mission fields'), and secondly, the explanation that this was due, not to any fault in the essential message of Christianity, but to the Western cultural garb in which it had hitherto mainly been presented. Rightly or wrongly, it was concluded by some Christians that the Gospel would be heard and accepted if it could only be clothed in some cultural garment other than that tailored somewhere along the North Atlantic axis. That this 'contextualisation' theory was at the same time able to make common cause with third-world dislike of transnational companies, and with various types of 'liberation theology' to produce a number of indistinct pressure-group or class-bound theories of religion (black, red, feminist, 'a Gospel for the poor') is all too understandable, on these premises. To the extent that such groups as these actually feel themselves to need a religious foundation, it is practically inevitable that they will use religion chiefly as a mark of separate identity. It is less inevitable that those who seek to influence them religiously will use the same arguments; but that they are being used, consciously or unconsciously, in this way is one aspect of today's world picture.

With this we may at the same time compare the remarkably

successful attempts made in recent years by a number of Asian religious movements to gain a following in the West. Those originating in India (Transcendental Meditation, Hare Krishna and others) have actually produced a type of religion carefully contextualised, that is, tailored to the needs of young people alienated from what they take to be the roots of western religion and culture. Since the hectic 1960s, their attempts at contextualisation (which may seem to be mainly a matter of marketing) have been remarkably successful.

Nevertheless there is a considerable difference between the culture of, say, present-day India as it actually is, and those detached fragments of that culture which the Neo-Hindu movements have marketed for Western consumption. Willy-nilly, on coming to the West, these movements have been forced to adapt to a Western context, just as Christianity, in its modern journey east, gradually assumed characteristics which Western Christians did not always understand, and of which they often did not approve. There is to my mind an inevitability about this process (in whichever direction) which the student is well placed to observe, given openness and insight. Attempts to *force* religion into a predetermined cultural model are on the other hand seldom successful, if for no other reason than that the model is static, while cultures are not. Given time, any religious tradition can, if it wishes, learn to accommodate itself to any culture – whether in the priestly or the prophetic, a positive or a negative sense. But force-fed, greenhouse-type contextualisation I suspect will always remain a talking-point among theorists, while most ordinary believers (blessedly few of whom are intellectuals) will contextualise simply by doing what comes naturally.

Meantime, if the mystics' claims are true, and they are actually achieving oneness with the Ground of all Being, far beyond the shifting sands of culture, there is little the student can do but to treat their statements with respect. In the end, he may have to leave them to their visions and ecstasies; for after all, he can study only what they say, and not the Reality to which they constantly refer. But if they say anything at all, they use language – and language is a powerful cultural implement.

One suspects, however, that the greater part of religion is far more culturally conditioned than most believers realise. What there is of the treasure of religious Truth comes in the earthen vessels of Culture. The attempt to distinguish between the one and the other may be difficult, and it may occupy the normal person for his allotted three score years and ten. But it is a quest well worth pursuing, and in the last resort, it has provided the subject matter, not only of this little book, but of the written and unwritten libraries of the whole of the study of religion.

Epilogue

The two quotations which I have placed after the title page of this book say something important about the motivation for the study of religion, as I have attempted to describe it. The quotation from John Donne's third *Satyre* dates from the 1590s, that is, two decades or so before his ordination. Its central two words are 'doubt wisely': extreme views on religion, either for or against, 'may all be bad'; the traveller on an unfamiliar road must learn to ask his way, and is urged to avoid the extremes of total indifference on the one hand, and the precipitate rushing off in the wrong direction on the other. Donne was even then no enemy of the truth, though he had no very high opinion of some of those who claimed that they had actually found it. Truth, he said, stands 'On a huge hill, Cragged, and steep, ... and hee that will Reach her, about must, and about must goe ...'

Over and over again I have had to say that there is a difference between those who, in studying religion, say in effect, 'This is divine revelation', and those others who say no more than 'This has been believed to be divine revelation'. In addressing myself entirely to the latter proposition, I have by no means wished to rule out the former – though there will certainly be those students (and others) who will probably read what I have written in that light. To all students, therefore, I offer Donne's words, that belief does not have to be either good or bad of itself, but that if the student has to doubt (as most do) let him at least 'doubt wisely'.

The other quotation comes from Charles de Brosses, and was first published in 1760. Paraphrased, it says that the student's business is not with what, in matters of religion, people *might* do or *ought* to do, but what they *actually* do, and the ways in which they actually behave. This is a principle for which, where religion is concerned, many appear to show very little understanding. It is absolutely crucial for the serious student. Of course it does not mean that he should have no ideals, be a total relativist, or maintain an attitude of chilly detachment in face of every phenomenon studied. What it does mean, on the other hand, is that the serious business of scholarship begins with the attempt to see clearly what is already there in the world of religion, past as well as present, abroad as well as at home. If this task is shirked – as it has so largely been shirked in the past – then there will always be a great gap in our knowledge, not necessarily of God, but of ourselves.

A couple of years ago, an American reviewer of the BBC TV world religion series *The Long Search* made an unfavourable comparison between that and Sir Kenneth Clark's earlier *Civilisation* programme. He did not actually call *The Long Search* amateurish, but he did draw attention to the painfully elementary nature of the questions which it raised in comparison with those brought up in the previous series, and suggested that in point of understanding, the BBC evidently felt it safest to assume nothing. Conrad Hyers' words are worth quoting. He wrote:

> ... that this type of host and program should have been produced by the same BBC which had produced Kenneth Clark's *Civilisation* suggests something of the longer search most westerners have to go through in dealing in a sophisticated and knowledgeable way with the variety of religious forms that are very much a part of the twentieth century. (*Theology Today*, April 1979: 83).

In a sense, of course, the BBC was entirely right in directing its programmes toward the average viewer, and in engaging a 'plain man' as host. The viewing public cannot know what it has either never been taught, or refuses to learn. But it is sad nevertheless that where there is no much to be seen and so much which awaits understanding, doubt should be equated not with wisdom but with wickedness; inquiry with eccentricity; and the attempt to understand with the diversions of the academic ivory tower. Donne and de Brosses knew better. For our part, it may be that there is no more serious intellectual – and perhaps spiritual – enterprise in which we can engage at this present time than the serious attempt to achieve an understanding of religion. Admittedly it may be more of an ideal than an attainable actuality, and I for one hope that I am under no illusions as to its difficulties. If faith were the whole of religion, then probably there would be no other path worth following than Augustine's 'believe in order to understand'.

But religion, as we have been discussing it, is not only faith, but all the direct and indirect consequences to which faith leads – all that mankind has ever done which refers itself to a final transcendental authority in matters both temporal and spiritual. And it is the nature of this notion of ultimate authority, and the consequences to which such a belief leads, that we know far too little about. Authorities we know; but in their controversies and dismissals we have learned to doubt, not wisely, but scornfully, impatiently and fiercely.

Of course there are a host of practicalities connected with the 'how' of the study of religion with which this book has not attempted to deal. In these pages I have been mainly concerned with the question 'why' – a question which I may or may not have succeeded in answering. Let me finally, however, express my deepest intentions in some words culled from Francis Bacon's essay on *The Proficience and Advancement of LearningDivine and Humane* (1605):

> I do foresee likewise that of those things which I shall enter and register as deficiencies and omissions, many will conceive and censure that some of them are already done and extant; others to be but curiosities and things of no great use; and others to be of too great difficulty and almost impossibility to be compassed and effected ... I shall be content that my labours be esteemed but as the better sort of wishes, for as it asketh some knowledge to demand a question not impertinent, so it requireth some sense to make a wish not absurd.

References

(books and articles quoted in the text)

Acquaviva, S.S., 1979, *The Decline of the Sacred in Industrial Society* (ET), Oxford: Blackwell.

Berger, P.L., 1967, *The Sacred Canopy*, New York: Doubleday.

Butterfield, H., 1960, *International Conflict in the Twentieth Century*, London: Routledge & Kegan Paul.

Campbell, C., 1972, *Toward a Sociology of Irreligion*, New York: Herder & Herder.

Churchill, W.S., 1959, *My Early Life*, London: Collins (Fontana).

Cook, S.A., 1914, *The Study of Religions*, London: Adam & Charles Black.

Cox, H., 1965, *The Secular City*, New York: Macmillan.

Dodd, C.H., 1947, *The Authority of the Bible*, London: Nisbet.

Durkheim, E., 1915, *The Elementary Forms of the Religious Life* (ET), London: Allen & Unwin.

Eckardt, C.R., 1968, *The Theologian at Work*, London: SCM.

Eliade, M., 1978, *No Souvenirs* (ET), London: Routledge & Kegan Paul.

Fallding, H., 1974, *The Sociology of Religion*, Toronto: McGraw-Hill.

Forsyth, P.T., 1915, *Religion in Church and State,* London: Hodder & Stoughton.

Galloway, G., 1935, *The Philosophy of Religion*, Edinburgh: T. & T. Clark.

Geden, A.S., 1922^2, *Comparative Religion*, London: SPCK.

Geertz, C., 1965, 'Religion as a Cultural System,' in Banton (ed.), *Anthropological Approaches to the Study of Religion*, pp. 284-338. London: OUP.

Knox, R.A., 1950^2, *A Spiritual Aeneid*, London: Burns, Oates.

Knox, R.A., 1952, *The Hidden Stream*, London: Burns, Oates.

Kraemer, H., 1938, *The Christian Message in a Non-Christian World,* London: Edinburgh House.

Kristensen, W.B., 1954, *Religionshistorisk studium*, Oslo: Norli.

Leclerq, J., 1962, *The Love of Learning and the Desire for God* (ET), New York: Mentor.

Leuba, J.H., 1912, *A Psychological Study of Religion*, New York: Macmillan.

Lewis, C.S., 1960, *Studies in Words*, Cambridge, U.P.

Menzies, A., 1922[4], *History of Religion*, London: John Murray.

Nock, A.D. (ed. Stewart), 1972, *Essays on Religion and the Ancient World*, London: OUP.

Nehru, J., 1956[4], *The Discovery of India*, London: Meridian Books.

Pratt, J.B., 1920, *The Religious Consciousness*, New York: Macmillan.

Radhakrishnan, S., 1960[11], *The Hindu Way of Life*, London: Allen & Unwin.

Sharpe, E.J., 1965, *Not to Destroy but to Fulfil*, Lund: Gleerup.

Sharpe, E.J., 1975, *Comparative Religion: a History*, London: Duckworth.

Sharpe, E.J., 1978, *Universal Religion for Universal Man*, Melbourne: ANZSTS.

Smart, N., 1968, *Secular Education and the Logic of Religion*, London: Faber.

Smith, W.C., 1963, *The Meaning and End of Religion*, New York: Macmillan.

Smith, W.C., 1967, *Questions of Religious Truth*, London: Gollancz.

Spiro, M.T., 1965, 'Religion: Problems of Definition and Explanation,' in Banton (ed.), *Anthropological Approaches to the Study of Religion*, pp. 85-126, London: Tavistock.

Troeltsch, E., 1923, *Christian Thought: its History and Application* (ET), London: University of London Press.

Underhill, E., 1930[12], *Mysticism*, New York: Dutton.

Vermes, G., 1962, *The Dead Sea Scrolls in English*, Harmondsworth: Penguin.

Whitehead, A.N., 1926, *Religion in the Making*, Cambridge U.P.

Whitehead, A.N., 1933, *Adventures of Ideas*, Cambridge U.P.

Whitehead, A.N., 1954, *Dialogues of Alfred North Whitehead* (ed. Price, L.), London: Reinhardt.

Yinger, J.M., 1970, *The Scientific Study of Religion*, London: Macmillan.

Zaehner, R.C., 1966, *Hindu Scriptures*, London: Dent.

Index